For You

Volume 1: Summary
Volume 2: Derivation
Volume 3: Constitution
Volume 4: State Organisation
Volume 5: Digital
Volume 6: Media
Volume 7: Labour
Volume 8: Planned Economy
Volume 9: Social Market Economy
Volume 10: Barter Economy
Volume 11: Free Market Economy
Volume 12: Finance
Volume 13: Innovation
Volume 14: Education
Volume 15: Health
Volume 16: Infrastructure
Volume 17: Security
Volume 18: Justice
Volume 19: Foreign Affairs
Volume 20: Integration
Volume 21: Family

Andreas Seidl

Handover of Power

Global Version

Volume 20: Integration

Imprint

Bibliographic information of the German National Library:
The German National Library lists this publication in the
German National Bibliography; detailed bibliographic data
are available on the Internet at http://dnb.dnb.de.

© 2022 Dipl. Pol. Theodor Andreas Seidl

Cover: Christiane Ebrecht
Translation: DeepL, Cologne
Production and publishing: BoD – Books on Demand,
Norderstedt

ISBN: 978-3-7568-0073-5

Acknowledgements

My thanks go to my family and friends who have made me who I am today. Special thanks to all those who supported me in writing this book. I would like to thank all my classmates, teachers, fellow students, lecturers, demonstrators, activists, colleagues, companies and countries with whom I have had the privilege of sharing the experiences from which all the ideas in this book have emerged. I would like to thank the staff of Books on Demand for their kind helpfulness. I thank the citizens of Seligenstadt for the harmony and solidarity in which I was able to write.

Foreword

This policy concept contains a variety of proposals for possible political reforms. It can be peacefully and democratically adapted to any current political system of any state in the world, but also to political systems in families, clubs, associations or companies. Wherever humans make or submit to rules that manage living together, the following proposals can be helpful. Readers who find the proposals so helpful that they would like to implement them together with like-minded people can contact the author. The contact form on the last page can be used for this purpose.

Faults and defects
I ask for your understanding that this volume was not professionally proofread. I could only afford professional proofreading for the summary. Spelling errors and unfortunate phrasing may therefore occur. As soon as this volume has sold enough to pay for a professional proofreading, it will be done. After that, a new edition will be published.

English version
Please understand that this volume has been translated automatically. I could only afford a professional translation for the summary. Poor wording and spelling errors may therefore occur. In case of doubt, the German version shall prevail. As soon as this volume has sold enough to pay for a professional translation, it will be done. After that, a new edition will be

published. It was more important to me that no one in the world should have an information advantage than individual translation errors in the complete work.

References
If something has been quoted directly, it is set in italics. If the headings contain footnotes, the sources for direct and indirect quotations apply in the chapter for which the heading stands. Otherwise, quotations or source references are directly at the word or at the end of the sentence or paragraph. This book contains parts of text based on the Federal Constitution of the Swiss Confederation of 18 April 1999 (as of 12 February 2017), abbreviated to BV[1] and the Constitution of the Canton of Bern of 6 June 1993 (as of 11 March 2015), abbreviated to KV[2] .

If the constitutional paragraph, or individual paragraphs thereof, are based in whole or in part on extracts from the BV or KV, this is indicated in a footnote. The references to the corresponding footnotes for constitutional paragraphs are usually found after the heading of the affected chapter and sometimes in the body of the text. Articles used in the Swiss constitutions are listed in the footnote with a number after the title of the constitutional paragraph. Example: §123 Sample title: BV Art.123, KV Art.123.

All internet sources are fully cited in the footnotes. They were last accessed on 30.09.2021. All literature sources are also listed in full in the footnotes.

All references to tasks undertaken by other ministries and described in more detail there are given in footnotes. Example: Model Ministry - 1.2.3 Model Chapter.

All footnotes are to be viewed in comparison to the respective source, so-called indirect quotations. Direct quotations are set in italics, but hardly ever occur. The source reference is intended to enable further investigation and to take copyright

---

1 This is not an official publication. Only the publication by the Swiss Federal Chancellery is authoritative. https://www.fedlex.admin.ch/eli/cc/1999/404/de On 14.12.2021

2 This is not an official publication. The Bernese Official Collection of Laws is authoritative. https://www.belex.sites.be.ch/frontend/versions/2420?locale=de#ART71 On 16.12.2021

into account.

Table of contents
1 Goals of the Ministry of Integration 13
2 Departments 14
2.1 Central Department 14
2.1.1 Staff 14
2.1.2 Organisation 15
2.2 Management Department 16
2.3 Integration Department 16
2.4 Immigration Department 17
2.5 Asylum Department 17
3 Tasks of the Ministry of Integration 18
3.1 Change in the areas of responsibility in the future 20
3.1.1 Short term 21
3.1.2 Medium term 21
3.1.3 Long term 22
4 Citizenship and aliens law 22
4.1 National 22
4.2 Foreigner 23
4.2.1 Tourist 24
4.2.2 Guest 24
4.2.3 Naturalised foreigner 25
4.2.3.1 Naturalisation test 26
4.2.3.2 Naturalisation phase 26
4.3 Status changes 27
4.4 Residents' Registration Office 28
4.4.1 Identity cards 29
4.4.1.1 National ID 30
4.4.1.2 Child ID 30
4.4.1.3 Asylum ID 30
4.4.1.4 Guest ID 30
4.4.1.5 Foreign citizen ID 31
5 Integration Agency 31
5.1 Indoor service 31
5.2 Field service 33
5.2.1 Integration Office 34
6 Integration 35
6.1 Official languages 36
6.2 Demography 37
6.3 Cultural protection area 38

6.3.1 Freedom. 39
6.3.2 Security 40
6.3.3 Special rules 40
6.3.4 Emergence and dissolution. 41
6.4 Religious communities 42
6.4.1 Church tax. 43
6.4.2 Places of worship 43
6.4.3 Law books in places of worship 44
6.5 Religion management 44
6.5.1 Secularism 44
6.5.2 Loyality to the constitution 45
6.6 Speed of integration 46
7 Immigration. 46
7.1 Rights and duties. 46
7.2 Residence 47
7.3 Integration Committee 47
7.4 Quota of foreigners 49
7.4.1 Voting questionnaire for nationals 49
7.4.1.1 Maximum number 50
7.4.1.2 Integration or assimilation. 50
7.4.1.3 Full employment. 51
7.4.1.4 Number of asylum seekers. 51
7.4.1.5 Number of refugees. 51
7.4.2 Questionnaire for foreigners. 52
7.4.3 The following measures 52
7.5 Immigration conditions. 53
7.5.1 Entry conditions for economic forms 54
7.5.2 Guest work. 55
7.5.3 Capital export 56
7.6 Immigration procedure 56
7.6.1 Entry 57
7.6.1.1 Data entry. 57
7.6.1.2 Searching for accommodation. 57
7.6.1.3 Examinations at the embassy. 58
7.6.1.4 Identity card at the Residents' Registration Office 59
7.6.2 Hometown. 59
7.6.2.1 Guided tour 60
7.7 Integration measures 60
7.7.1 Language tuition 60

7.7.2 Integration troop 61
7.7.3 Immigrant festival 61
7.7.4 Integration bus. 62
7.7.5 Integration theatre 63
7.7.6 Civil defence lessons. 64
7.8 Integration Directory 65
7.8.1 Admission 65
7.8.2 Profile. 66
7.8.3 City selection 67
7.8.3.1 Domestic characteristics 68
7.8.3.2 Selection by immigrants 68
7.8.3.3 Display of matching cities 69
7.8.3.4 Avoidance of parallel societies 69
7.8.4 Invitation to the integration theatre 70
7.8.5 Statistics on the quota of foreigners 70
7.9 Departure procedures 70
7.9.1 Voluntary return. 71
7.9.2 Forced return 72
7.9.3 Deportation 72
7.9.4 Readmission. 74
7.9.5 Lack of nationality 75
8 Asylum. 76
8.1 Asylum Committee. 76
8.2 Reception capacities 77
8.3 Asylum Directory 78
8.3.1 Asylum Directory website. 79
8.3.2 Views 80
8.4 Asylum procedure 81
8.4.1 Financing. 82
8.4.1.1 Asset management. 83
8.4.1.2 People's Bank online account. 84
8.4.1.3 Asylum Village real estate bonds 85
8.4.1.4 Cryptocurrency. 85
8.4.2 Responsibilities. 86
8.4.3 Asylum application. 87
8.4.4 Entry of asylum seekers .88
8.4.5 Initial recording 89
8.5 Refugees 90
8.5.1 Host family 91

8.6 Asylum seekers 92
8.6.1 Asylum Village 92
8.6.1.1 Move. 92
8.6.1.2 Utilities 93
8.6.1.3 Compulsory education 93
8.6.1.4 Community 94
8.6.1.5 House building 94
8.6.1.6 Development plan. .95
8.6.1.7 Owner. 96
8.6.1.8 Completion. 96
8.6.1.9 Reintegration of asylum seekers. 97
8.6.1.10 Domestic economy 97
8.6.1.11 Professionals 98
8.6.1.12 Foreign trade. 98
8.6.1.13 Cultural bazaar 98
8.7 Departure 98
8.8 Punitive measures 99
9 Switching to the new system. 100
9.1 Statistical recording. 100
9.2 Withdrawal of domestic nationality. 100
9.3 Stop of the admission .101
9.4 Deportation waves. 101
9.4.1 Citizens of Member states of the Continental Union
. 102
9.5 Compensation payments. 102
9.6 Integration of foreigners 103
9.7 Resettlement of asylum seekers 103
9.8 Waves of refugees 103
9.9 Conversion of the old ministries 103
Contact form 107

1 Goals of the Ministry of Integration

The Ministry of Integration aims to facilitate friendships between humans and to reduce and avoid hostility. In order to promote friendships, fellow citizens should be able to understand each other. The Ministry of Integration helps residents overcome cultural, religious or linguistic boundaries and creates niches where such boundaries can be used to protect identity. The former is achieved through Immigration, Integration and Asylum procedures, the latter through Cultural Protection Areas and Asylum Villages.

The Ministry of Integration aims to measure the speed of integration of the population and immigrants as accurately as possible in order to adjust its performance to the agreed maximum speed. The speed of integration is measured by the statistical queries to determine the quota of foreigners. The aim is to ask the domestic population whether foreigners are allowed to immigrate and, if so, how many.

The aim of immigration policy is that only humans immigrate inland because they love the country and its people. For this, the Ministry of Integration offers a naturalisation procedure. For humans who want to immigrate for economic purposes, it offers visas for guest workers. For humans who want to immigrate out of necessity, there is the asylum procedure. The aim is to ask immigrating foreigners whether they want to stay or return.

The Ministry of Integration pursues the long-term goal of preserving the human races and enabling peaceful coexistence between all human species. We humans are still lucky to be one species and all races can produce fertile offspring together. The long-term goal is to keep the human gene pool diverse and thus more resilient. The human gene pool becomes more resistant to diseases and environmental influences through racial diversity and thus better ensures the survival of the human species. Breeds have the opportunity to protect themselves through cultural protection areas.

2 Departments

The departments are divided into sub-departments and enumerations are usually considered as their individual units. Many tasks of some departments are completely taken over by other ministries as a service.

2.1 Central Department

Part of the Central Department is the Reception Office with the Courier and Mail Room, which directs all concerns, broadcasts and visitors to the appropriate place in the ministry.

2.1.1 Staff

The Human Resources Department is responsible for staff development and planning. For this purpose, it takes care of the recruitment of junior staff, intern and trainee programmes as well as the selection procedures for employees and special selection procedures for applicants with disabilities. For politicians and employees, the department prepares a job plan. In all its tasks, it works in voting with the personnel board.[1]
All other personnel matters are transferred to the respective ministries. The Ministry of Education is responsible for the training and further education of employees for the state service.[2] The Ministry of Labour takes over the service law.[3] This includes the labour and collective bargaining law for employees in the state service, remuneration, personnel administration of all careers and employees, flexitime, holiday and sickness records, working time with or without flexitime in part-time or full-time at the place of work or in home work. The Ministry of Infrastructure provides housing assistance for all state employees.[4] The Ministry of Finance's Pay Office takes care of employees' salary, expenses, travel and relocation

---

1 Ministry of State Organisation - 2.1.1.1 Personnel board
2 Ministry of Education - 2.1.1.1 Education and training for the state service
3 Ministry of Labour - 4 State enterprises, 13 Labour Directory
4 Ministry of Infrastructure - 2.1.1.1 Housing assistance for state service employees

costs.[5]

The Ministry of Education provides childcare for all employees in the state service.[6]

The Ministry of Health is responsible for the occupational health service.[7] It ensures occupational health management, deals with the treatment, education and prevention of occupational accidents, controls and provides occupational health and safety through the health auditors[8] of the Company Auditing Agency[9].

2.1.2 Organisation

The ministries of media, security, justice, finance, labour, state organisation provide audit services for quality management in the ministry, evaluation of work performance, revenues and expenditures, as well as corruption prevention, sabotage protection and, if necessary, disciplinary matters.[10]

The Ministry of Labour regulates procurement law and ensures corruption-free state orders and procurement.[11] The Ministry of Finance organises the annual budget vote and ensures proper accounting in each ministry.[12] It regulates budget procedures, budget law, staff budgets, departmental budgets, costs and cash management, and assists ministries in budget planning for the budget vote. The language service for translating talks or texts is provided by the Ministry of Education.[13]

The Ministry of Digital Affairs supports the supply of Information Technology.[14] In voting with the Procurement Office of the Ministry of Labour, it takes care of the

---

5 Ministry of Finance - 2.1.1.1 Staff remuneration
6 Ministry of Education - 2.1.1.2 Childcare for state service employees
7 Ministry of Health - 2.1.1.1 Occupational Health Service
8 Ministry of Labour - 20.7.2 Health auditor
9 Ministry of Labor - 20 Company Auditing Agency
10 Ministries of Media, Security, Justice, Finance, State Organisation - 2.1.2.1 Audit services
11 Ministry of Labour - 6 Procurement Office
12 Ministry of Finance - 8 state revenues, 9 state expenditure
13 Ministry of Education - 2.1.3 Language Service
14 Ministry of Digital Affairs - 2.1.2.1.1 Supply of Information Technology

procurement, provision, maintenance and service of technical devices and software. Much of this is produced in-house to ensure data protection in information and communication technology. Information technology and digitalisation officers audit and advise the ministries. Digital appointment calendar and documentation services are provided as well as a digital policy archive including a library.

2.2 Management Department

The Management Department is the minister's department. With his office team, he provides policy planning and analysis for his ministry and coordinates the relationship between the nation and the municipality through exchanges with his deputies in the municipalities. He initiates cooperation with other ministries or citizens in committees and is supported by the Ministry of State Organisation.
The Ministry of Media Affairs, through its media service, provides press and public relations for the ministry, moderates civil dialogue, trains or provides a spokesperson for the minister, writes speeches and texts on request, and ensures the implementation of conferences and events.[15]
The Ministry of Digital Affairs is responsible for digital management and thus provides departmental management. It automatically produces business statistics, staff surveys and the current state of research through statistics. It automatically forwards proposals to the affected or empowered state employees. In document management, it ensures digitalisation and that ministries share forms with each other.[16]

2.3 Integration Department

The Integration Department formulates draft legislation for the rights and obligations of nationals and foreigners in voting with the Minister of Integration. The Integration Department monitors compliance with nationals' and foreigners' laws and

---

15 Ministry of Media Affairs - 2.2.1.1 Media Service
16 Ministry of Digital Affairs - 2.1.2.1 Digital Service

uniform requirements for the residence and naturalisation of foreigners based on these laws. In this regard, it supervises the Residents' Registration Offices and the Integration Agency. It monitors voting on official language, demographic development and cultural protection areas. In cooperation with the ministries of security and justice, it ensures that law enforcement and jurisprudence are adapted within the cultural protection areas. It supervises the religious communities for compliance with the requirements and adherence to the constitution.

2.4 Immigration Department

The Immigration Department formulates the bills on residence and handling of immigrants in voting with the Minister of Integration. It oversees the voting on the quota of foreigners and the integration committees. In cooperation with the ministries of economy, it ensures compliance with immigration conditions and, with the ministries of foreign affairs and security, with entry and departure procedures.
It provides integration measures and cooperates with the Ministry of Education for language classes, with the Ministry of Security for the integration troop, civil defence classes and the integration bus, with the Ministry of Infrastructure for the Immigrant Festival and with the Ministry of Media Affairs for the Integration Theatre. For the selection of a suitable place of residence and the organisation of integration measures, it operates the integration directory[17] .

2.5 Asylum Department

The Asylum Department formulates draft legislation in the asylum procedure in voting with the Minister of Integration and in the asylum application procedure in voting with the Minister of Foreign Affairs.
In cooperation with the ministries of Foreign Affairs, Security, Finance, Planned Economy and Infrastructure, it oversees the

---

17Ministry of Digital - 12 Directories

asylum process from application to deportation. It accounts for all services and ensures that the Asylum Villages are financed in a balanced or profitable manner. It oversees the reception capacity and accommodation in the Asylum Houses of the Social Villages and in the Asylum Villages and Host Families. It operates the Asylum Directory on the intranet and internet in cooperation with the Ministry of Digital Affairs. Punitive measures taken by the Integration Agency must be approved by the Asylum Department.

3 Tasks of the Ministry of Integration

The Ministry of Integration has the task of ensuring that the population is as peaceful and amicable as possible and of creating areas for the protection of minorities. In the broadest sense, the task of the Ministry of Integration is to keep the risks of globalisation for the people as low as possible. If risks cannot be avoided, they should be clearly named and thus assessable for all participants.

The Ministry of Integration is responsible for regulating who is granted domestic citizenship, when and how long foreigners are allowed to stay as tourists and guests, what foreigners have to do to become naturalised, and how the status can change. It creates a naturalisation test and sets requirements for the naturalisation phase. It operates the Residents' Registration Office, where nationals, children, asylum seekers, guests and naturalised persons obtain and renew their identity cards. The Integration Agency provides the necessary statistics on the speed of integration, immigration and moves, organises the interaction between ministries and citizens, and implements measures for integration. It operates integration offices in the town halls for this purpose.

Regardless of nationals, the ministry has the task of ensuring the integration of the population segments. In voting with the population, it ensures that the population grows, stays the same or shrinks by managing immigration. Language, religion and other cultural characteristics may vary among the population. The Ministry of Integration's task is to avoid tensions between them. To this end, it designates a single official language that applies throughout the country. Subcultures that wish to exclude themselves or meet with resistance from the rest of the population can express themselves among their own kind in cultural protection areas. The Ministry of Integration regulates the necessary freedom and security to implement special rules in cultural protection areas in cooperation with the Ministries of Security and Justice. It is the task of the Ministry of Integration to ensure the separation of church and state, to examine religions for their conformity with the constitution and, if necessary, to restrict or ban them.

The Ministry of Integration regulates and manages immigration in voting with the population. The quota of foreigners determines how many foreigners are allowed to immigrate to the country as a whole and to each individual municipality. Through voting questions on integration and assimilation, domestic citizens and foreigners are asked whether they prefer to adapt to each other or to existing conditions. Foreigners also indicate whether they would like to return to their country of origin in the future or see their new homeland inland. The Ministry of Integration's task is to manage immigration in such a way as to ensure full employment.

Through immigration conditions such as impunity, ability to pay and entry conditions for the economic forms, it protects the population from criminals and social fraudsters, the economic forms from hostile takeovers, domestic citizens from wage dumping and domestic purchasing power from the outflow of funds abroad.

The immigration procedure enables foreigners and domestic citizens to find their suitable new place of residence and quickly become at home in the new city. The procedure is accompanied by integration measures that are mandatory for naturalisation. Domestic citizens can attend the measures voluntarily or offer measures themselves. The Ministry of Integration offers digital support for domestic residents and immigrants during the move with the Integration Directory.

Should problems arise in the coexistence between immigrants and domestic residents, it is the task of the Minister of Integration to hold an integration committee. In addition to immigration, the Ministry of Integration is also responsible for the regularisation of exit procedures. It can call on foreigners to leave voluntarily, force their departure or deport foreigners. Readmission and handling of missing nationals is handled in cooperation with the Ministry of Foreign Affairs.

The asylum procedure is also carried out in cooperation with the Ministry of Foreign Affairs. While the Ministry of Foreign Affairs is responsible for the asylum application procedure, the Ministry of Integration takes care of the residence of asylum seekers inland. In voting with the people, it determines the reception capacities and the asylum procedure in detail in an asylum committee. Asylum seekers finance their stay by building houses. They live in Asylum Villages which they have built and whose real estates are sold for profit after their departure. The Ministry of Integration works together with the Ministry of Infrastructure for this purpose. The Ministry of Integration's task is to prepare asylum seekers for their return in the best possible way. They are accommodated with asylum seekers who speak the same language and come from the same region if possible. In this way, they should be able to make friends and learn how to set up entrepreneurial communities or cooperatives in their home country. In organising the Planned Economy way of life in the Asylum Village, the Ministry of Integration is supported by the Ministry of Planned Economy. Once the country of origin is safe again, the Ministry of Integration organises the departure of all asylum seekers.

The task of the Ministry of Integration is to give asylum seekers the opportunity to become naturalised domestic citizens. For this, it depends on the willingness of voluntary domestic citizens who agree to act as host families for these asylum seekers until they are naturalised.

3.1 Change in the areas of responsibility in the future

The Ministry of Integration has unchanging tasks and those that differ in the short, medium and long term. The unchanging tasks include the operation of the Residents' Registration Offices and the Integration Agency. In addition, immigrants, whether from foreign countries or within the country, are to be familiarised with the domestic population. Immigration is adapted over time to the change and dissolution of national borders in order to accompany the communitarisation of states with suitable integration policies.

3.1.1 Short term

In the short term, only immigration from International Union member states is possible until all domestic citizens of the International Union have been naturalised and the standard of living in all member states has converged to 95%. In this phase, the So-called "continental fortress" is the guideline, which ensures internal cohesion between the peoples of the continent and seals itself off from immigrants through quotas of foreigners for this discovery phase. Quotas of foreigners are supposed to represent the speed of integration, the maximum speed of which must be adapted to the will of the people in order for integration to succeed. As soon as hereditary enmities between the peoples of the continent have disappeared, the integration of further cultures can be permitted.

3.1.2 Medium term

In the medium term, the first member states of the International Union have merged to form the unified states of the Continent, so that increasingly foreigners are becoming domestic citizens of a larger federal state. Ethnic cultures and traditions have a chance to survive in cultural protection areas. The quotas of foreigners for citizens of the continental International Union are increasingly disappearing, and as soon as the population is ready, third-country nationals can increasingly immigrate. In the medium term, immigration is allowed as long as there is full employment and all inhabitants have a similar standard of living, measured by the price level. The price level may fluctuate by a maximum of 5%.

3.1.3 Long term

In the long term, there will be no more immigration, only migration, because borders have disappeared in the united states of the world. The Ministry of Integration is limited to integration assistance between domestic and newcomers.

In the long term, the Ministry of Integration will continue to be responsible for ensuring cultural peace between the humans who can live where they want in the united states of the world. The Ministry of Integration ensures transparency of the cultures and religions represented in a city so that all residents know what manners and traditions they are dealing with locally. Here, when registering at the Residents' Registration Office, existing cultural groups in the immediate neighbourhood are pointed out and information is conveyed about what is important to people of that culture and what could lead to misunderstandings because it is so contrary. The only restrictions are the cultural protection areas, where residents are allowed to decide which culture or ethnicity is allowed to live and work in the limited area.

4 Citizenship and aliens law

The Ministry of Integration is responsible for legislation on nationals and foreigners as well as citizenship and naturalisation law. This distributes rights and obligations for domestic citizens and foreigners in a fair manner that promotes peaceful coexistence.

4.1 National[18]

The Ministry of Integration regulates in the nationality law who is granted national citizenship and thus becomes those entitled to vote as nationals. Those who have the domestic nationality are nationals. All nationals together form the national citizenship. All nationals living together inland on the basis of the domestic constitution constitute the national people. Every national has full voting rights to participate in all the political processes of his or her state. Therefore, he is

---

18 §246,4-6 Naturalisation

considered a member of the state in the literal sense.

Nationals living abroad cannot participate in voting and co-determination via the intranet unless they enter and visit an intranet café to do so. There is no provision for postal voting. Lending out the voting right to a self-selected delegate[19] , on the other hand, is possible at any time.

In principle, the nationality is not divisible. Anyone who holds the domestic nationality cannot hold any other nationality. This condition is justified by equality of voting rights. In international law and intergovernmental treaties or in an International Union[20] , the peoples affected are always asked to vote. Persons with dual nationality could then vote twice, which violates the democratic principle of equal voting rights for all participants. Moreover, this also discriminates against humans with only one nationality because they have fewer rights and freedom of choice.

A human is granted the national citizenship at birth if both parents are nationals. Children of whom only one parent has domestic nationality are granted the nationality of the foreign parent. They can opt for domestic nationality from the age of ten and at the latest until they reach the age of majority.

4.2 Foreigner[21]

The Ministry of Integration regulates immigration to the inland and residence in the inland under the law on foreigners. Foreigners who wish to enter the inland require a permit to do so. This permit can be granted either through an approved asylum application, a visa or an agreement between the inland and the country of origin of the foreigner. The Ministry of Foreign Affairs is responsible for issuing these permits in voting with the Integration Agency.

The residence permit is not withdrawn from those who remain unpunished and can support themselves. If foreigners have taken out state social insurance in the Social Market Economy, they receive at most social benefits to the extent of

---

19 Ministry of State Organisation - 8.6.4.4 Delegates
20 Ministry of Foreign Affairs - 5.8 International Union
21 §40.2 Acquisition and loss of civil rights: BV Art.38

their contributions. In the Free Market Economy, insurance companies offer unemployment or social insurance with their own insurance conditions.

Living on the street is not possible, and begging is also forbidden. If foreigners are unemployed, they must find accommodation with friends or family. Children of foreigners can be supported in the Children's House[22] in the Social Village for a maximum of 12 months if their parents are unemployed, but they can also stay with their parents if the best interests of the child permit. Foreigners who live without income or savings for more than 12 months must leave the inland within a period of 3 months.

The right of residence inland ends immediately for every foreigner if he becomes a criminal or insolvent. Insolvent means no longer able to support oneself financially and no longer able to pay for the return journey to one's country of origin. Criminal means having committed at least three minor offences or one serious offence punishable by detention. This is followed by deportation within one month. Those who resist are liable to detention for the amount of the search costs and will be deported after working off[23] the costs in detention.

4.2.1 Tourist

Foreigners who stay in the inland for less than 12 months without working or renting a property here are considered tourists. Tourists are free to move, shop and stay in domestic accommodation. A hostel must be registered as a company and can be mobile or at a fixed location. The entrepreneur is obliged to register the accommodation of a tourist in the Travel Directory.

---

22 Ministry of Planned Economy - 18.1.7 Children's House
23 Ministry of Justice - 7.5 Detention, 7.5.10 Labour

4.2.2 Guest

A guest is a foreigner who wishes to live in the inland for longer than 12 months and for a maximum of 10 years. Foreigners who wish to become a guest must obtain permission to do so from the embassy in their home country, unless their home country is in an International Union with the inland or has agreed to visa exemption. Foreigners who wish to work or rent accommodation inland must be recognised guests. Each guest must declare a planned date of departure, which may be postponed up to 2 times, but may not be longer than 10 years after the first entry as a guest. A guest who wishes to live inland for more than 10 years may be naturalised if he or she passes the naturalisation procedure and the quota of foreigners allows it.

4.2.3 Naturalised foreigner[24]

In the naturalisation law, the Ministry of Integration regulates how foreigners can become naturalised persons and thus obtain permanent residence. Foreigners who wish to reside inland indefinitely must become naturalised within a maximum of 10 years. To do so, they must pass a naturalisation test and successfully complete a naturalisation phase. The integration authority checks all the necessary documents. It also checks how high the quota of foreigners is in the country as a whole and admits more or fewer foreigners for naturalisation accordingly. In case of doubt, those foreigners who have better test results and have been able to meet the requirements of the naturalisation phase to a greater extent are naturalised. If successful, the Integration Agency grants permission to issue an identity card for naturalised persons.

As naturalised persons, foreigners are granted permanent residence permits and electoral and voting rights for statistical purposes. Naturalised persons have a work permit in the Social Market Economy and Free Market Economy, but not for the Free Market Economy and Barter Economy. They do not have the right to become criminals or insolvent.

---

24 §246.1 Naturalisation

4.2.3.1 Naturalisation test[25]

The naturalisation test requires a final examination tailored to knowledge of the national language, work ethic, virtues, religious character, past, constitutional fidelity and criminal laws, but also asks about general basic arithmetic, writing and reading skills. Another compulsory part is the final test of civil defence instruction. If this test is not passed, the theoretical and practical part must be attended for at least three months in an educational institution in order to be allowed to repeat the final exam. The naturalisation test is prepared in cooperation with the Ministry of Education. Those who fail the naturalisation test up to 3 times must immediately name a date of departure within the next 12 months or will be deported after three months at the latest if they don't name the date. Those who cannot pay for their deportation must work off the price of return in detention. Foreigners who immigrate to the inland with their children must obtain the parenting licence within 9 months.

4.2.3.2 Naturalisation phase

Those who want to become naturalised go through a naturalisation phase. This phase lasts 5 years on average, but it can also be completed more quickly or more slowly. However, the maximum duration is 10 years. There are written and oral exams at local schools and universities, as well as proof of work performance, friendships, club memberships and honorary service over the course of at least 24 months, but no more than 10 years. Thus, anyone who has too few domestic friends, incurs debts or has not remained in a club for at least 12 months or has never engaged in honorary service for at least a total of 2 months, does not speak the national language perfectly and has remained unpunished cannot be naturalised. For refugees living in host families, the host family is sent a questionnaire. In it, they are supposed to give grades from 1 to 6 for social behaviour, among other things. A list of faults can also be given. It contains bad manners that the refugee has

---

25 §246.2 Naturalisation

acquired or lost over time. These assessments are also included in the final rating.

The foreigner himself must submit the following proofs to the Integration Office. Either the marriage certificate with a nationals or the signatures on the motivation letters of at least 10 friends, half of whom must be naturalised persons and half nationals, must be submitted. There must also be confirmation from a club through a written testimonial of at least one year's membership. At least one testimonial of current employment must be submitted or, in the case of self-employment or employer employment, a testimonial must be provided by means of an anonymous People's Computer survey[26] of clients, providers or employees. The place where honorary service was performed must issue a testimonial about the time. All honorary service periods must add up to at least 2 months. The testimonials must certify at least sufficient performance to successfully pass the naturalisation phase. Lastly, at least one national citizen must be present as an advocate at the final interview at the Integration Agency.

4.3 Status changes[27]

Status changes may occur when nationals change or requirements are no longer met in order to maintain a certain status.

Nationals who adopt a foreign nationality automatically lose their domestic nationality. Naturalised persons who become criminals or insolvent immediately lose their residence permit and have to leave the country in due time. Guests can become naturalised persons if they pass the naturalisation test and the naturalisation phase. Foreigners can become asylum seekers if they fulfil the asylum application procedure[28] . Asylum seekers can decide to become refugees and be naturalised as refugees if they meet all the requirements. Children with one foreign and one national parent can decide once between the age of ten and the age of majority to take on the national citizenship

---

26 Ministry of Digital Affairs - 13.6 People's Computers
27 §40.1 Acquisition and loss of civil rights: BV Art.38
28 Ministry of Foreign Affairs - 9 Asylum application procedures

and give up the foreign citizenship. Tourists become guests if they stay inland for more than 12 months. The prerequisite for this is that the visa is sufficiently extended or a temporary residence permit is granted in order to be allowed to live and work in the inland.

4.4 Residents' Registration Office[29]

The Ministry of Integration is responsible for the registration law and the registration system. It maintains offices in the town halls and uses the Persons Directory for data management. There is a Residents' Registration Office in every town hall. This is where identity cards are issued and updated. The Residents' Registration Office closest to the location of the People's Computer is responsible. Citizens can change their address in the Persons Directory. Citizens can have their People's Computer automatically located by means of a location function in order to update the address data. Before an automatic address change, citizens must confirm the new entry by clicking on it.

The Residents' Registration Office reports to the Statistical Office[30] how many humans are in the country. Only the Residents' Registration Office can open profiles in the Persons Directory at birth or close them after death. Foreigners are obliged to report their current place of residence to the Residents' Registration Office.

The Residents' Registration Office ensures freedom of movement and settlement in the country. Nationals may restrict freedom of movement in cultural protection areas for certain groups of people. Freedom of settlement is only available to domestic nationals; foreigners may settle wherever the quota of foreigners has not yet been met. Hotel accommodation is exempt from this.

---

29 §22 Freedom of movement, §23 Freedom of establishment: BV Art.24
30 Ministry of Digital Affairs - 6 Statistical Office

4.4.1 Identity cards

The Ministry of Integration regulates in the identity card (ID) law which person receives which identity card or has to carry it. The Residents' Registration Office is where the identity cards are issued. This is also where all measures of identification are taken in order to be able to identify the person effectively. These are photographs of the face with a 3D camera, fingerprints, iris and signature. This data is stored at the Residents' Registration Office and on the identity card. Identity cards and passports are issued at cost plus 10% profits and are renewed every 10 years. Every 10 years, images are taken with a 3D camera, fingerprints, signature and iris are renewed.

All identity cards are expelled with additional functions. They serve firstly for identification, secondly as an electronic means of payment of the People's Bank[31] with the limit of the account balance, thirdly as an access card for the intranet in the intranet café or for the People's Computer and fourthly as a Health Card with all medical examination results.

All identity cards look similar. They contain the same information about a person, but are labelled differently in the title field and have a different background colour. The information about a person is the passport photo, surname, first name, date of birth, place of birth, nationality, eye colour, height, signature and, if applicable, the artist's name or name of the order. If an address is available, it is entered, otherwise the intranet address of the profile in the Persons Directory is given. The identity card also shows the issuing country and the city where the expulsion was made, as well as a number. The number is different for each identity card and is only issued once. This prevents forgeries.

Foreigners who are tourists, transients or suppliers for an inland delivery are not issued with an identity card, but identify themselves with the passport of their country of origin.

---

31 Ministry of Finance - 11 People's Bank

4.4.1.1 National ID

Nationals are issued the national identity card and a passport. The passport is the travel document for nationals and is issued and renewed together with the identity card. As long as nationals are minors, they receive the child ID card and a passport. Once they are of age of majority, they receive the national identity card. The national identity card has all the necessary memory chips in the card to vote anywhere inland. The face, fingerprints and iris are stored on the memory chip for recognition by voting computers or People's Computers.

4.4.1.2 Child ID

Children receive the child ID card from birth until the age of majority. The picture, fingerprint and iris are renewed every 5 years. Nationality is recorded and stored on the identity card. Foreigner children thus have the right to vote for statistical purposes for the ministries of education and family from the age of ten.

4.4.1.3 Asylum ID

Asylum seekers and refugees receive an asylum ID as long as they enjoy asylum inland. The asylum seeker's country of origin is also noted on the card. With the asylum identity card, an asylum seeker receives restricted access to areas of the intranet that are necessary for asylum seekers and refugees. Before departure, the asylum ID must be returned to the Residents' Registration Office.

4.4.1.4 Guest ID

Guests receive a guest ID card as long as they are staying inland. The date of departure and nationality are also noted and stored on the identity card. They must carry it with them in order to be able to identify themselves if necessary, i.e. during police checks. They can also use their passport for this purpose, but this does not give them the functional possibilities of the domestic identity card. When leaving the country, the guest ID must be returned.

4.4.1.5 Foreign citizen ID

Naturalised persons receive a foreign citizen identity card as soon as they have successfully passed the naturalisation test and the naturalisation phase, and as long as they remain unpunished and solvent. They present all the tests they have passed at the Residents' Registration Office and then receive their identity card. The identity card will also show and record their nationality. The identity card must be handed in at the Residents' Registration Office as soon as the criminal offence or insolvency has occurred.

5 Integration Agency[32]

The Integration Agency is responsible for clarifying fundamental questions of migration and integration policy raised by domestic residents, immigrants, travellers, ministries and other states. It acts in accordance with the laws of the Ministry of Integration. It is responsible for information and communication with the immigration authorities of the member states and the municipalities. It keeps statistics in the field of migration and asylum to calculate the quota of foreigners. The field service records the number of foreigners and the moves of nationals between two municipalities. These data are collected by the field service and forwarded to the indoor service and the Statistical Office to initiate measures if necessary.[33]

5.1 Indoor service

The indoor service deals with all matters of migration and integration policy at national and international level. This includes networking with all necessary ministries and their

---

32 §188.5 Statistics
33 Ministry of Digital Affairs - 6 Statistical Office

institutions.

Agreements on uniform standards are being prepared with the ministries of migration and tourism of other Continental Union member states and data is being cross-checked. The agreements must be brought into force by the Minister of Integration or by referendum. Data matching includes all persons travelling through Member States and nationals of one Member State residing or working in another Member State.

Necessary requirements for immigrating or entering foreigners are agreed with the domestic ministries of family, education, infrastructure, foreign affairs, labour, economy and finance and forwarded to the field staff in the integration offices for implementation. The indoor service coordinates the cooperation of all integration offices in the municipalities. Uniform standards and exceptions are thus agreed upon or reviewed.

The indoor service records the number of foreigners living inland and in the municipalities individually in order to calculate the quota of foreigners in the country and the individual municipalities. It reports the result to the field service and compares the current numbers with the permissible maximum number. Using the data from the indoor service, the field staff can distribute foreigners to municipalities. The requirement is that the quota of foreigners should be similar throughout the country, unless a municipality has set a higher or lower quota of foreigners for its municipality. The indoor service is responsible for compliance with the national quota of foreigners and the field service is responsible for compliance with the municipal quota of foreigners.

The indoor service also monitors all cultural and religious communities for their compliance with the constitution and promotes the exchange of information with the population. The field service is responsible for on-site support and control. In legal matters, the indoor service can ask the Integration Council for clarifications or draft legislation. The Integration Council consists of the Minister of Integration and his municipal deputies.

5.2 Field service

The field offices are the integration offices in each town hall. The field service handles all affected national citizens, influxes, immigrations, emigrations and deportations of foreigners and works with Customs to do so. Concerned or committed citizens with a low or high speed of integration can report to the field service to voice their concerns. As soon as a new building area is to be expelled, the field service must organise a municipal committee[34] to draw up a socially acceptable building plan in voting with the citizens of the municipality. The development plan stipulates how quickly how many residential or commercial properties may be built. The local population should determine for themselves how quickly they are able to integrate a certain number of new residents into their local community.

New citizens moving to a city receive information and registration options for integration measures, clubs and events to help them find friends and places of interest in the new city more quickly. The field service records which municipality the citizens moved from and why they moved. Depending on the reason, policy measures may be necessary, such as better integration of locals into the local population if they are lonely, or the construction of a new day-care centre if the reason for the move is the desire to have children. When building a day-care centre, the field service would have to forward the data to the Education Authority[35] . This shows that the field service, based on its data collection, can instruct the indoor service to start cooperation with other ministries in order to be able to implement a policy content. The short official channel is permissible, but must be accompanied by a data transfer in order to avoid surplus or shortage. Using the nursery school as an example, the field officer could also go directly to the Education Authority in the neighbouring office in the town hall. It is crucial that the step is documented so that it is clear that a registered need of citizens is to be met, which is decisive for the legal basis of the action and the financing of the measure. The indoor service is responsible for

---

34 Ministry of State Organisation - 9.6 Committee
35 Ministry of Education - 4.5 Education Authority

avoiding shortages, for example when concerns accumulate in many municipalities but only a few affected people report in individual municipalities.

Emigrants are asked about their reasons before they emigrate. If resentment of the departing homeland is the reason for emigration, this reason is noted and reported to the indoor service. If possible, a solution should be found with the disgruntled emigrant. If this is not possible, the case must be included in the statistics of emigrants due to dissatisfaction. If the Ministry of Integration is not responsible for the dissatisfaction, the case is forwarded to the Federal Moderator's Office .[36]

Foreigners are also given advice and checked on how and whether they fulfil all the necessary requirements. If there are foreigners in a municipality who are obliged to leave the country, the field service must summon them to the Integration Office to arrange their departure plans. If necessary, the police can be instructed to search for the person. In the event of a search and arrest, the affected person is placed in detention pending deportation by Customs.

5.2.1 Integration Office

The Integration Office is responsible for tourism, culture, religion and the integration of foreign newcomers in the city. Tourists, newcomers and domestic residents can obtain information here and obtain and network offers from tradespeople in the tourism industry, clubs and event organisers. The Integration Office administers all naturalisation and integration measures of a municipality and mediates with affected foreigners. Foreigners only need to visit the Integration Office to obtain the necessary advice and forms for successful integration.

36Ministry of State Organisation - 4.4 Federal Moderator's Office

6 Integration[37]

Integration means creating social cohesion with equal living conditions and enabling the preservation of regional and cultural identity.

Intergovernmental integration is based on ministries of several states strengthening their cohesion through uniform and common laws. Through federalism, they can distribute their responsibilities between municipalities, nations and International Unions. Through subsidiarity, they can hand over their responsibilities to one of the three political levels best suited for this purpose.

Interpersonal integration is based on humans adapting to circumstances or to each other. Adapting to circumstances means assimilation and adapting to each other means integration. The Integration Agency has the task of reconciling both possibilities by allowing the local population to decide whether newcomers should adapt to the conditions in the municipality or whether the municipality also wants to adapt to the newcomers. Municipalities that want to prescribe conditions must formulate the conditions in a committee with the deputy minister of integration. The same applies to foreigners arriving inland, except that the Minister of Integration and the people are responsible for formulating the conditions in a committee. The Ministry of Integration takes care of the necessary laws and their implementation. The fewer the requirements, the more integration is possible, and the more requirements, the more assimilation is necessary.

National and municipal committees determine what is considered a general national cultural property and what cultural property is only produced or practised in certain municipalities. In a municipal voting, municipalities can declare themselves cultural protection areas where subcultures exclusively share their cultural property. In order to meet the requirements of individual municipalities, the local Integration Office organises and promotes cultural events and integration measures that are adapted to the requirements of the municipality. The deputy integration minister of the municipality is responsible for implementation.

37§184.4 Promotion of music, sport, film, culture and art: BV Art.69, §190.9 Environmental protection: KV Art.32

6.1 Official languages[38]

Citizens and companies have freedom of language. They may speak the language they wish to speak to each other. However, when speaking or writing in state institutions and with government personnel, a valid official language must be used. Those who do not speak it must provide a translation. Interpreters can be requested by the persons affected through the office. Those who do not speak the official language must pay for translation services themselves.
Language is considered the highest cultural asset of humankind. Language shapes the humans who speak it. The number of foreign words in the vocabulary testifies to foreigner influence in the population that speaks the language. Grammar shapes the lifestyles of the speakers. Knowing these facts, the Ministry of Integration, in voting with the people, regulates the design of the official language. The official language inland is the national language. In order to keep the language understandable for all inhabitants, foreign words for which there are domestic words should be avoided as far as possible. This applies to all state workers and to anyone while working on the orders of the state. Municipalities may designate another language as their official language to enable their citizens to maintain their cultural identity. Dialects are explicitly included. The unification of states usually leads temporarily to another official language. A new language must be developed for a new federal state, made up of components from the member states and voted on together with the new people.[39] Before the new language may be introduced as an official language, 95% of the nationals must be able to understand and speak it.
In order to represent the genders fairly in official language, general statements about persons of any gender are formulated in the gender form of the author. This makes it clear which gender the author is. If several genders are involved in the formulation, they can agree on one gender or use the mixed form, such as citizens.

---

38 §16 Language-free: BV Art.18, §185 Languages: BV Art.70
39 Ministry of Foreign Affairs - 7.3.4.4 World Language

6.2 Demography

The people decide on the demographic state of the population. Each woman does this with the help of her personal birth rate. All women of childbearing age thus decide whether the people shrink, grow or remain the same size, age or rejuvenate. The Integration Agency collects this data and can prompt the Integration Minister to convene a People's Committee. This is to clarify with the people whether they would like to shrink, grow or stay the same. It is the task of the Ministry of Integration to abolish this discrimination against men and to enable them, as part of the people, to have a corresponding say, which has been taken away from them through the renunciation of violence and contraceptives. According to the will of the people, immigration can be conditional, increased or decreased. For example, if a majority favours a higher birth rate, only women of childbearing age may immigrate until the agreed birth rate is reached.

Through the birth rate and immigration, the ministries of education, labour and economy can adjust early to the coming number of workers and consumers to avoid surplus or shortage and ensure full employment.

As long as the people do not stipulate otherwise, the Ministry of Integration, in cooperation with the Ministry of Family Affairs, motivates the nationals to have a birth rate of 2 children per woman in order to keep the population constant. Children in the country should be trained as well as possible by identifying needed strengths and letting the child, as a learning human being, decide what his or her strengths are most suited to. Inland, foreign parents must also grant this right to their children, which is a permissible interference in their freedom of upbringing for the benefit and will of the child.

Especially the children of naturalised persons should be free to decide whether they want to fall in love with the national society and stay here, and to father children with nationals in order to give their children the choice of nationals.

6.3 Cultural protection area[40]

Through cultural protection areas, humans as living beings should have the opportunity to create niches in which groups can set themselves apart and live in their own way without causing damage to others. The constitution applies everywhere and its requirements for cultural protection areas must not be exceeded. Accordingly, physical, mental and financial integrity must be guaranteed everywhere in the country. Every human being may move freely everywhere as long as no law or property right prohibits him or her from doing so. In cultural protection areas, at least unharmed passage must be allowed. Cultural protection areas may only be designated by nationals. Takeover by another country must be avoided.

Cultural protection areas come into being as soon as 75% of the citizens of a municipality or a city support an initiative quorum of the same name. In a subsequent municipal committee, the conditions and requirements are negotiated by all citizens of the municipality. In a subsequent voting, at least 90% of the residents of the future cultural protection area must vote in favour. The turnout for this voting must not be less than 60%.

In designated places, for example, the Bavarian, homosexual, vegan, Salafist or similar way of life is then practised. All residents and visitors to the municipality abide by this. Each cultural protection area writes on its place-entry sign what is permitted, desired or not desired. At the village entrance sign, everyone knows whether they want to or are allowed to shop, go on holiday, work or live there. This data is also published in the Integration Directory. Violations are punished by the security agencies with a warning the first time, and with an expulsion the second time, which can be extended to a certain period and the entire cultural protection area.

More discrimination is allowed in the cultural protection area than elsewhere. Globalisation also means migration and consequently integration or assimilation. In certain cases, assimilation may be impossible and result in discrimination

---

40§22 Freedom of movement, §37 Cultural protection areas, §130,1,3,4 Cultural protection areas and economic zones: BV Art.50, §186 Peaceful Separation

and exclusion. This consequence is accepted within the boundaries of the cultural protection area in order to protect minorities. Minorities should thus be able to preserve their way of life.

6.3.1 Freedom

Cultural protection areas serve to guarantee nationals the greatest possible freedom to live out their cultural inclinations without endangering social peace. Therefore, cultural protection areas may have laws that exclude other humans and restrict their fundamental right to freedom of movement or, for example, economic, religious or linguistic freedom. Fundamental rights that may not be restricted without the explicit consent of each individual affected are the rights to physical, material and financial integrity.

In cultural protection areas, residents' behaviour can be more restricted to certain behaviours. For example, drug use can be declared illegal by municipal law, or only belief in a religion can be specified. As can be seen, this can make legal acts outside the cultural protection area illegal and illegal acts legal in the cultural protection area.

Legal acts that become illegal may only be punished with punitive measures with which the affected resident agrees. If he does not agree, he must immediately move out of the cultural protection area and a re-entry ban may be imposed.

Illegal acts that become legal must be done with the consent of those affected and must not damage or disadvantage third parties and the environment. The municipal law legalising illegal acts must include a sufficient protection concept for humans and nature outside the cultural protection area. In case of doubt, the people may veto[41] or repeal quorum legalising laws and amend them in a committee with the inhabitants of the cultural protection area and adjust, prevent or abolish them by a final referendum.

---

41 Ministry of State Organisation - 9.5.14 Veto quorum

6.3.2 Security

Humans who break the rules in the cultural protection area may only be punished by the security forces, vigilante justice is not permitted under any circumstances. The monopoly on the use of force remains with the people and thus with the ministries of security and justice, which cannot be placed under municipal self-government. Any violation by organised vigilante justice is considered a coup attempt. The security forces and the judicial officers of the ministries of security and justice watch over the observance of the laws of a cultural protection area and punish violations. At the same time, they ensure that the constitution is respected and that humans outside the cultural protection area are not negatively affected.

6.3.3 Special rules

To ensure that everyone knows what they are getting into when they enter the cultural protection area, the specific laws and codes of conduct are listed on the entrance signs to the town and in the Integration Directory, and can be viewed as a separate code of law in the Law Directory[42] . To the extent and for as long as necessary, visitors of residents, suppliers or transients who do not comply with the requirements may still enter the cultural protection area. Residents may make arrangements to avoid entry by undesirable persons as far as possible by specifying other places to visit, adjusting delivery routes or travel routes.

Transport routes may run through cultural protection areas, which would require a significant diversions for people passing through. Residents must establish bypasses or tunnels in these cases to preclude trespassing. Transportation routes such as state highways or railways where there is no exit or stop shall remain unaffected or must be rerouted underground or above ground at the expense of the residents of the cultural protection area. The route must not become more than 10% longer as a result of the bypass.

For deliveries of goods, shipping centres can be established at

---

42 Ministry of Justice - 4.7 Law Directory

the entrance to the village where deliveries are received and picked up by residents. Residents can be forced to receive or host certain visitors only outside the cultural protection area.

6.3.4 Emergence and dissolution

A minority can move into a city specifically to make it a cultural protection area, or they already form the majority there. The population there does not have to move out, even if they are in the minority. Offering compensation for moving out is possible, as is refusing the offer. Domestic residents who do not want to accept the innovations and cannot or do not want to comply with the new rules must not be forced to do so. A minority that becomes a majority in a cultural protection area must, for its part, also uphold minority rights there. Because in a cultural protection area the right for certain groups of people to move there can be restricted, long-term appropriation is possible.

A cultural protection area may extend to a region as soon as surrounding towns are sufficiently populated with like-minded people. This region may not exceed 5% of the total area of the country. All cultural protection areas together may not exceed 25% of the country's area. A veto quorum can be used to increase or decrease the percentages of the available land area. In this voting, those entitled to vote can indicate numbers and at least 65% of the people must agree. A reduction below 0.1% is not permitted.

If the inhabitants of a cultural protection area pursue an expanding and appropriating policy to increasingly more parts of the country, the people can dissolve cultural protection areas. As soon as several cities, several regions or a national area of more than 0.5% are affected by the policy of a particular cultural protection area, a veto quorum is possible. In the following committee, the extension is discussed and rated. In the following voting, at least 65% of the population must decide in favour of the dissolution of one or more cultural protection areas. At least one cultural protection area must remain for the minority.

A cultural protection area with a decreasing population is

dissolved as soon as the number of inhabitants decreases by more than 25% compared to the time of the voting that led to the establishment of the cultural protection area. Residents of a cultural protection area may own a maximum of 2 real estates. They may live in both properties or rent out one property.

The Minister of Integration may dissolve cultural protection areas if their inhabitants pose a danger to the general public. A danger to the general public exists if the threat or use of psychological, physical or financial coercion is made without the consent of those affected. If citizens do not agree with the resolution by the Minister of Integration, they can negotiate the decision through a veto quorum in a committee and have it voted on by the people.

The aim is to prevent a minority from spreading its ideology by buying up properties, resettling and depopulating in order to corner the majority. As soon as the minority becomes a majority, it does not need cultural protection areas, but determines the policy and the former majority can survive in cultural protection areas. This makes fluid change possible in the long term and eradication impossible.

6.4 Religious communities[43]

If a religious community wishes to establish or operate places of worship inland, it must obtain permission from the Integration Agency. After a check for constitutional fidelity and if no signs of a sect are discernible, religious communities are approved. In the first step, preachers must be trained at state colleges inland. For this purpose, a religious community can open chairs at state colleges, which it must finance and whose curriculum it determines in voting with the Integration Agency.

Religious communities may advertise for members, give religious instruction, hold sermons or other religious events. It must be possible to join or exit at any time. Coercion to become or remain a member is considered coercion, extortion

---

43§12 Freedom of faith and conscience: BV Art.15, §187,1,2,4
Separation of church and state: BV Art. 72

or exploitation and can be charged to the religious community as a religious offence. Religious communities may be obliged to hold joint meetings with other religious communities and to care for regular exchanges in order to reduce historical enmities.

6.4.1 Church tax

Religious communities may apply to the Ministry of Integration for an account with the People's Bank. If the religious community proves that it is faithful to the constitution, the account will be opened at the People's Bank by the Ministry of Integration. All members of the religious community must go to the town hall and update their identity card with the new religious affiliation at the expulsion terminal there. Here they are asked whether a transfer standing order will be established for the tax account. In addition to the state taxes, the inflows to the private account are then taxed. The amount is determined by each religious community itself. This service is subject to a fee for religious communities. The price is based on the provision costs plus 10% profit.
Religious communities can also merge in order to be able to do even more good with their tax revenue. In this case, they have to apply to the Ministry of Integration and then get a new joint account at the People's Bank.

6.4.2 Places of worship

Places of worship are all buildings in which religions hold their meetings and organise sermons or prayers. Houses of worship must in principle be open to all humans in the country, otherwise the religion is considered a sect. A specific dress code or separation of genders is permitted, but not the exclusion of certain persons or groups of persons. In all places of worship, preaching and praying must be done in the national language so that everyone present can understand the sermon or prayer.

6.4.3 Law books in places of worship

The domestic constitution must always be available in printed form in all places of worship and prayer. The edition must not be older than 5 years after the last amendment. A tablet PC with an internet connection to the current website of the domestic laws can also be used for this purpose, but it must then contain the Constitution, the Civil Code and the Criminal Code.

6.5 Religion management

Once a year, the representatives of all religious communities authorised inland meet with the Minister of Integration and his deputies for talks in the Integration Council or in the context of a People's Committee on the street and on Government Television. Here, citizens and religious representatives can voice praise, suggestions and criticism and try to bring about changes that are acceptable to the majority. The requirements for secularism and adherence to the constitution, and which religious community successfully implements them or violates them, serve as a basis for discussion.

6.5.1 Secularism[44]

There is a complete separation of church and state. Only the people make laws for themselves and are free from any religious determination. Every citizen is bound only by his or her moral conscience. How and where this moral conscience is formed or shaped is up to each citizen. Religions have no right to influence policy and are considered an undemocratic pastime subject to freedom of faith and conscience. Religious assertions that cannot be scientifically substantiated and offices that decide on a municipality but are not directly elected are not capable of meeting the demands of a modern democratic state. The state is therefore prohibited from outsourcing state services to religious communities and from influencing their political structures, processes or contents.

---

44 §187.3 Separation of Church and State

6.5.2 Loyality to the constitution[45]

No one-sided political opinion may be expressed in sermons and prayers. Preachers who support the policies of certain parties or party wings and reject others are committing incitement of the people[46] . Religious communities are prohibited from rating the politics of the day far from their religious scriptures and traditions. Due to one-sided politicisation in an undemocratic environment, such as religion with preachers as non-democratically elected leaders, repeated incitement of the people in several places of worship by several preachers is considered promotion of extremism and attempted coup.[47] The religious community's licence can be withdrawn in that case.[48]

Comprehensive school students from ethics classes regularly attend and record meetings, sermons and prayers to learn about the religious communities around them. The protocols are forwarded to the Integration Agency and checked in cooperation with the civil police. The protocols count as a performance record for the learners and must be handed in digitally. They are automatically checked and reported to the Civil Police and the responsible Integration Office in case of suspected violations.

The field service, in cooperation with the civilian police, randomly, covertly and unannounced checks the religious embassies for constitutional compliance during a sermon, prayers or religious gatherings. Covert video recordings are made as evidence. If violations of the law have been committed, the preacher is publicly and unannounced informed of the offence during the next sermon in front of his municipality by an employee of the Integration Office and the evidence is shown. Preachers are warned on the first offence and must recant what was said unlawfully in a clarification. If this is observed again in a subsequent examination, the preacher will be charged with incitement of the people. If offences are committed in the name of a religion, all preachers of

---

45§187.2 Separation of Church and State: BV Art. 72
46Ministry of Justice - 8.9.8 Incitement of the people
47Ministry of Justice – 8.14.5.3 Coup
48Ministry of Justice - 8.9.7Religious Offences

the municipality from which the offender comes are given occupational bans.

In cases where an auditor observes that the entire municipality is unlawful, the religious community can also be classified as a local sect and thus prosecuted under criminal law.[49]

6.6 Speed of integration

The speed of integration is measured in generations. It indicates how willing a person is to get to know foreign cultures and persons, to accept new cultures and habits and to incorporate them into their own habits. The higher the readiness, the faster the speed of integration of this person and vice versa. Usually, the speed of integration of a person remains similar and tends to decrease with increasing age. The Ministry of Integration is responsible for measuring the above-mentioned readiness of all persons who want to live in the country or immigrate. Through its agencies, it ensures that humans with similar speeds of integration can live together and know what the speed of integration is in their place of residence.

7 Immigration[50]

The Ministry of Integration is responsible for immigration legislation. This regulates entry, departure, residence and settlement. This includes moves between two municipalities and immigration from abroad.

7.1 Rights and duties

Immigration is connected with certain rights and obligations, which differ for nationals, nationals of Continental Union member states, nationals of states with which the inland has a corresponding agreement and nationals of other states.

Domestic nationals can manage immigration from abroad and take advantage of all state services before and after a move. Nationals of Continental Union member states enjoy

---

49 Ministry of Justice - 8.9.6 Sects
50 §243.1 Legislation on foreigners and asylum: BV Art. 121

the right of free movement to live and work anywhere on the continent. They do not need a visa and are granted naturalised persons status with all its rights and obligations without having to go through a naturalisation phase. In the course of communitarisation[51] , further continental harmonisation is taking place in the law on foreigners, bringing the rights and obligations of all Continentals into line. Nationals of states with which the inland has an agreement do not need a visa to live, work or take a holiday in the inland. They become guests immediately if they intend to stay longer than 12 months. Nationals of other countries need a visa for entry into the inland. When applying for a visa, they are obliged to state whether they intend to holiday, live or work inland.

7.2 Residence[52]

The right of residence is temporary for all foreigners as long as they are not naturalised and it is limited by the condition of exemption from punishment and ability to pay.
Foreigners are denied the right to buy land inland. As naturalised persons, they can rent or lease land and build, buy or rent real estate as long as they also reside inland themselves. The ministries of economic affairs may impose further restrictions.[53] If land is needed in the course of state land-use planning, leases can be extraordinarily terminated and properties located on the land can be expropriated. The Ministry of Infrastructure is responsible for such procedures and compensates those affected according to their loss.

7.3 Integration Committee

The Minister of Integration can convene a national integration committee and each of his deputies can convene a municipal integration committee in his municipality. The committee is convened as soon as a sufficient number of domestic citizens and foreigners complain to the Integration Office. The sufficient

51 Ministry of Foreign Affairs - 5 Communitarisation
52 §196,3,4 Spatial planning
53 Ministries for Economic Affairs - Real estate sector

number of complaints is 20% of the national or municipal population, which in this case means domestic nationals and foreigners. Therefore, no quorum can be triggered.[54] However, the procedure is identical to that of any quorum, except that foreigners have to register their complaint in person at the Integration Office. The protocol is the same as that of a usual quorum with a text entry field and is filled out by a field staff member of the Integration Agency.

At the Integration Congress, prejudices and problems between natives and immigrants or domestic nationals and foreigners are voiced, analysed and proposals for improvement are turned into legislative texts that are passed or rejected in national or municipal votes.

The People's Committee is broadcast in real time on Government Television[55] , the Citizens' Committee on Local Television[56] . The audience includes affected citizens from the whole country or municipality. The Minister of Integration or his or her responsible deputy is always present on the panel. Depending on the situation, politicians from cities with positive and negative examples are also present, as well as foreigner and asylum officers from the Integration Agency, police officers, prison guards, criminologists, youth centre directors from affected neighbourhoods and the rural region, pre-naturalisation test teachers, ethnologists, biologists, behavioural scientists, psychologists, social psychologists and foreigners from the lower and upper classes.

In the discussion, local residents or nationals say their prejudices or complaints first, followed by immigrants or foreigners. Afterwards, similarities and differences of culture are asked in the audience and an opinion is sought on which differences should be preserved or abolished. The specialists from the panel discuss the reasons and origins of the prejudices as well as their causes and effects with the speakers from the audience. The audience makes suggestions for improvement, which are rated by the panel and adapted if necessary to make them feasible.

---

54 Ministry of State Organisation - 9.5 Quorum
55 Ministry of Media - 7 Government Television
56 Ministry of Media - 9 Local Television

The drafted text is put to a vote of those entitled to vote as a law applicable nationwide or as a municipal law.

7.4 Quota of foreigners[57]

The determination of the quota of foreigners is connected with a statistical data collection. The necessary data is provided by nationals, foreigners and the Integration Agency. The Integration Agency provides data on the number of foreigners, including asylum seekers, living and working inland and in the municipalities. All nationals provide data on their perceptions of immigration in voting questionnaires. All foreigners indicate to the Integration Agency if or when they intend to leave the inland again.

Foreigners who come from member states of the International Union receive their own quota of foreigners, which is determined in a separate voting. The procedure corresponds to the determination of the quota of foreigners for all foreigners from other states.

The constitutional quota of foreigners is 20% for nationals of Continental Union member states and 5% of the total population of nationals for other foreigners.

7.4.1 Voting questionnaire for nationals

When and how often this voting is held nationally or municipally is decided by the domestics in a repeal quorum for the relevant national or municipal law or in a revision quorum for the constitutional article on the quota of foreigners.[58] The Minister of Integration, in voting with his or her deputies, may hold a newly national or municipal voting.

---

57 §188,5 Statistics, §244,2,3,7 Management of immigration: BV Art. 121a, §245 Quota of foreigners
58 §245 Quota of foreigners

7.4.1.1 Maximum number

All nationals vote on the number of foreigners they would like to see as a percentage of the total national population. The percentage indicates the proportion of foreigners measured against the total population of nationals. To facilitate voting, the number of the total population is displayed to the right of the input field. As soon as a percentage has been entered in the input field, the resulting permissible total number of foreigners appears to the left of the input field. Next to it, the current total number of foreigners is displayed.

This entry option is available for the whole country and for the municipality in which those entitled to vote live. Municipalities can thus allow an exception to the nationwide requirement within their borders. Municipalities can set higher or lower rates of non-nationals as long as the national average is not exceeded.

For the calculation, the place is selected, i.e. the whole country or a municipality, in order to record the number of nationals and foreigners living there. Now the number of foreigners is divided by the number of citizens and multiplied by one hundred. It is possible to measure this ratio at any time for all citizens in the Integration Directory. The voting results from all municipalities are decisive as to how high the maximum nationwide quota of foreigners may be. How high the nationwide quota of foreigners should actually be is determined by the results for the whole country. If there is a contradiction here, i.e. all those entitled to vote would want to admit fewer foreigners in their municipalities than they allow in the country as a whole, the nationwide quota of foreigners is adjusted to the lower value of those municipalities. This ensures that forced departures because the nationwide quota of foreigners has been exceeded are as rare as possible.

7.4.1.2 Integration or assimilation

Under the voting field for one's own municipality, the question is joined whether foreigners living there should integrate or assimilate. The meanings are listed under the question as a voting aid. Integrate means to mix the brought culture with the domestic culture and thus create a new mixed culture. Assimilate means to discard the culture brought with you and adopt the domestic culture in order to preserve the domestic culture. It also asks whether only immigrants who intend to return to their country of origin or who want to settle inland should settle here.

7.4.1.3 Full employment

In another question, those entitled to vote indicate whether immigration of foreigners should be linked to the quota of foreigners and also to full employment. This would stop immigration as soon as the unemployment rate exceeds 1%, no matter how much the quota of foreigners has been met.

7.4.1.4 Number of asylum seekers

In the penultimate question, those entitled to vote indicate the percentage of asylum seekers in relation to the total population of nationals. As a voting aid, the costs per asylum seeker are given above the input field. Below the input field, after entering the percentage, the total costs caused by this are displayed. The information to the right and left of the input field corresponds to the above information for foreigners.

7.4.1.5 Number of refugees

In the last question, those entitled to vote indicate the percentage of refugees in relation to the total population of their municipality. Above the input field there is the option of entering a number of refugees that one would like to accommodate. After entering the percentage, the minimum number of host families required is displayed below the input field. Those who are willing to volunteer as host families can enter their contact details in an input field after voting.

7.4.2 Questionnaire for foreigners

Foreigners are interviewed upon entry and can newly fill out the questionnaire up to 3 times at the Integration Office. They indicate whether they see their new homeland inland and want to stay here or if and when they want to return to their old homeland and with which conditions they connect their stay or departure. Conditions can be selected from a list of keywords. In the case of asylum seekers, this question results in them being accommodated either as an asylum seeker in an Asylum Village or as a refugee in a host family.
In another question, they indicate whether they would prefer to integrate or assimilate. This gives foreigners results on which municipality could become their possible new place of living because integration or assimilation is desired there.

7.4.3 The following measures

The voting results on the quota of foreigners give the Ministry of Integration the orders to implement the majority indications of the people and the affected citizens of a municipality.
If the number of foreigners approaches its maximum limit by 10%, no more foreigners are allowed to immigrate. Immigration is stopped and family reunification is also no longer possible. If the number of foreigners nevertheless increases, for example because foreigners have more than two children, foreigners are forced to move or depart or are deported.
If the quota of foreigners for a municipality is exceeded, sufficient foreigners must leave the municipality and move to a municipality with sufficient capacity or emigrate. If the quota of foreigners for the entire country is exceeded, calls for departure and, if necessary, deportation procedures follow.

7.5 Immigration conditions[59]

The basic condition for the immigration of foreigners is the quota of foreigners of Continental Union member states, asylum seekers and other foreigners throughout the country and the municipalities. The people manage this immigration independently and thus set conditions on maximum numbers and integration or assimilation. The Ministry of Integration is responsible for the rest of the management. It issues laws that regulate the conditions.

The Integration Agency examines and issues, limits or withdraws residence permits. The examination is carried out before the residence permit is issued and during the current residence permit. It checks whether the foreigner has been convicted of a crime by a final court decision, has abused social benefits, has sufficient knowledge of the national language, history, legislation and jurisprudence, as well as his ability to pay to support himself and his dependents. Different conditions apply to refugees, guest workers and voluntary immigrants.

Refugees whose asylum applications have been approved by the Ministry of Foreign Affairs are allowed to immigrate for a limited period of time. The time limit ends as soon as the country of origin is safe again. They are only granted a residence permit as a refugee outside a host family if they have been successfully naturalised, have remained crime-free for 3 years and if they have found a job in the Social Market Economy or Free Market Economy that could finance them and, if applicable, their family for 3 years.

Guest workers hired by a company in the Free Market Economy or Social Market Economy are allowed to immigrate for a limited period. The time limit ends as soon as the employment contract ends. The residence permit is granted if they have been able to finance themselves and, if applicable, their family for the last 3 years with their wages, have savings of at least 20,000 Dollars and have remained crime-free for the last 5 years.

All other foreigners who like to live inland because they like

---

59 §244,1,6 Management of immigration: BV Art. 121a, §246,3
Naturalisation: KV Art.7

the country, the people and the form of government are considered voluntary immigrants. They can immigrate for a limited period of time if they fulfil the following conditions. They must have savings of at least 200,000 Dollars, come to live inland without a criminal record and have passed the naturalisation test as a distance learner in their mother tongue.

7.5.1 Entry conditions for economic forms[60]

Foreigners wishing to immigrate to one of the four economic forms must fulfil different conditions depending on the economic form. The conditions consist of entry fees and naturalisation efforts. Entry fees are paid into the People's Bank account of the Integration Agency, which then transfers the money to the responsible Ministry of Economy. If guest workers are recruited and hired by domestic companies in the Free Market Economy and Social Market Economy, the entry fees are waived.

Foreigners are allowed to immigrate to the Free Market Economy who are guests and have to prove a solvency of 20,000 Dollars. The amount is deposited as a deposit with the People's Bank and paid out again on the day of emigration. It is used in the event of liability that the foreigner is unable to meet with his or her assets. If liability arises, the foreigner must leave the country within 4 weeks.

The Social Market Economy allows foreigners who are naturalised to immigrate and make a payment of 200,000 Dollars to compensate for missed years of contributions to compulsory insurance for past generations.

Foreigners who are naturalised persons are allowed to immigrate to the Planned Economy and make a payment of 1,000,000 Dollars to compensate for the missed contribution to past construction costs of all Social Villages. Immigration is not possible when capacity is full, and in the case of increasing capacity, foreigners must leave the Planned Economy until capacity is built accordingly.

Immigration into the Barter Economy is allowed for foreigners who are naturalised and make a payment of 500,000 Dollars

---

60 §244.6 Management of immigration: BV Art. 121a

to compensate for the missed assistance in the construction and care of all Barter Economy Zones. Should immigration jeopardise renewal capacity or come close to capacity limits, no more foreigners are allowed to immigrate or must leave the Barter Economy until capacity becomes available again.

7.5.2 Guest work[61]

Guest workers must obtain a labour migration visa in order to be allowed entry. The conditions for a labour migration visa are determined by the Ministry of Integration in voting with the Ministries of Foreign Affairs, Labour and Economic Affairs and the applicable law on employment permits for foreigners.

The number of labour migration visas issued may not exceed the permitted quota of foreigners in the municipality and the country. The term of each affected labour migration visa may be terminated by a Minister of Economy as soon as there is no longer full employment in the relevant sector. The term of all labour migration visas must be terminated by the Minister of Integration as soon as the unemployment rate rises above 3%. The origin of a guest worker does not play a role, i.e. whether the guest worker travels a long way and has to relocate or whether they are regular cross-border commuters on their way to and from work.

The employment of foreigners is only allowed in companies of the Free Market Economy and Social Market Economy. Their wages must be 10% higher than the standard wage in the Free Market Economy and 30% higher than the standard wage or minimum wage in the Social Market Economy. These wage duties go into the state budget as a tax and are used primarily for training and recruiting domestic labour. The wage must be sufficient to support the guest worker and, if necessary, his family.

To obtain a work migration visa, one must successfully apply to a company in the Social Market Economy or Social Market Economy and be allowed entry for an interview. Companies must give preference to domestic applicants over guest workers

61 §244.5 Management of immigration: BV Art. 121a

if they are equally qualified. If the application is successful, the applicant will receive the work migration visa with the same term as the employment contract. If the employment contract is for an indefinite period, the period ends when the employment contract is terminated by notice or dismissal. At the time of entry at the border post, the employer's confirmation must already be available. Provided the wage is sufficient to pay the local rent and cost of living for the specified number of persons, the persons may enter.

7.5.3 Capital export

Another condition for immigrant foreigners is to avoid exporting capital to support family or friends living abroad. This would be the case if foreigners working inland regularly remit money abroad. This act weakens domestic purchasing power and thus lowers the standard of living at home. Therefore, export duties are levied on foreign remittances to compensate for the loss of purchasing power. The Integration Agency checks compliance with the condition through automated control of account movements between immigrant foreigners and foreign accounts. financial institutions operating inland are obliged to transmit the data.

7.6 Immigration procedure

The immigration procedure is voluntary for nationals and compulsory for foreigners.

For all persons moving inland, the Ministry of Integration offers help before and after the move. Before the move, they can choose a place of residence where many residents share similar views or preferences. For this purpose, the Integration Directory offers the appropriate applications and the Integration Office offers personal assistance if necessary. After the move, newcomers can participate in integration measures that they can book through the Integration Directory or the Integration Office.

Immigrating foreigners use the same procedure, but must

first obtain an identity card and comply with the quota of foreigners and the requirement to integrate or assimilate.

7.6.1 Entry

Foreigners who want to immigrate inland must meet the immigration requirements and need a residence permit, an identity card and accommodation. Foreigners obtain all this before their entry at the embassy in their country of origin and through the Ministry of Integration's website. Foreigners who wish to apply for asylum follow the asylum procedure and can then take part in the immigration procedure if they wish to settle inland.

7.6.1.1 Data entry

The first step is for foreigners to create an admission and a profile on the embassy's website. To do this, they fill out the input mask for a profile in the Persons Directory, Labour Directory or, in the case of children, in the Education Directory and the Integration Directory. They must also state whether they intend to leave the inland again and specify a date of departure or whether they wish to remain in the inland indefinitely and become naturalised. Finally, they indicate whether they would prefer to integrate or assimilate and which cultural or religious preferences they care for.

7.6.1.2 Searching for accommodation

After entering the data, all necessary data is available to automatically search for suitable accommodation. Foreigners must use the Internet-based Integration Directory to find accommodation in their country of origin inland for themselves and, if necessary, also for their family. A programme shows the map of the inland and where the quota of foreigners is low enough to accept foreign immigrants and whether integration or assimilation is desired at the specified location. A link to the Real Estate Directory shows suitable houses or flats for rent or sale in the selected municipality. A link to the Labour Directory shows whether there are vacancies for the specified qualification in the vicinity. A link to the Education Directory shows where suitable educational institutions for the children are located in the vicinity.

The programme automatically calculates and displays all suitable places of residence. The foreigners select their favourite three places of residence and can automatically send enquiries and applications to sellers or landlords of real estate and employers. If only rejections follow, another three suitable places of residence can be selected and so on. Those who intend to start a company must prove that they can meet the immigration requirements of the selected economic form and pay a deposit of 25% of the amount.

7.6.1.3 Examinations at the embassy

In the second step, the foreigners send the results, together with the acceptance of enquiries and applications, to the embassy. The embassy translates the necessary information and sends the data to the indoor service of the Integration Agency. There, it is checked for the residence permit whether all immigration conditions are fulfilled. Depending on the purpose for which foreigners want to immigrate and whether this is possible at the specified place of residence is part of the verification of all personal duties from the first step. Another part is the verification of criminal convictions. The embassy asks the local Ministry of Justice for a certificate of good conduct of the foreigner listing all criminal offences committed and also sends it to the Integration Agency. Once all conditions have been successfully checked and are deemed to have been met, an appointment is made at the embassy. There, the foreigner must appear in person and present his passport. Any relatives who wish to immigrate with him or her must also fulfil all the conditions from the first step and appear in person at the appointment with their passport. At the appointment, fingerprints will be taken and photos of the face and iris will be taken, which will later be used to create the temporary identity card inland. Foreigners can indicate at which Residents' Registration Office they would like to pick up their temporary identity card. Finally, the Integration Agency issues the residence permit and a profile is created in the intranet-based Integration Directory and the Travel Directory. There it is noted until when the residence permit is limited.

7.6.1.4 Identity card at the Residents' Registration Office

In the third step, foreigners can enter the country and must report to the nearest border post, where customs officers confirm their entry in the Travel Directory.[62] There, foreigners are given an appointment at a Residents' Registration Office of their election, where they receive a temporary identity card as a guest, valid for 3 months. They can then use this identity card to conclude treaties inland, such as a sales contract, rental agreement or employment contract. The temporary identity card is to be carried as proof that the initial registration has already been completed and that the police know where the foreigner has to report to and by when in the event of a control. Once foreigners have found their place of residence and settled there, they must report to the local Residents' Registration Office within 3 months in order to obtain a proper identity card as a guest.

7.6.2 Hometown

Every new place of residence has the aspiration to become the new hometown for its inhabitants, where one can live peacefully and make good friends. All newcomers are therefore sent to the Integration Office after their visit to the Residents' Registration Office. There they receive all the information that tourists also receive and, in addition, all the offers for integration measures that exist in the municipality.

---

62 Ministry of Security - 8.2.5 Entry of foreigners

7.6.2.1 Guided tour

There is a guided tour for all newcomers as soon as 50 new residents have moved into the city. It is organised by the Integration Office. Volunteers from old and young residents who would like to offer a guided tour can report to the Integration Office. If there are not enough volunteers, the field staff takes over the guided tour.

7.7 Integration measures[63]

All integration measures are financed through taxes and are free of charge for all participants. Foreigners from countries outside the Continental Union must attend at least once; for all others, attendance is voluntary. The integration measures are designed to adequately present the cultural asset and its importance to the municipality and the nation. Particular emphasis is placed on whether integration or assimilation is desired in the municipality. Accordingly, integration measures for assimilation teach the domestic way of life and integration measures for integration teach how foreign and domestic ways of life can be bound together.

7.7.1 Language tuition[64]

Immigrants who are not yet fluent in the national language attend the national language classes of the local primary school in all grades at the same time. In order to be able to combine lessons with an appeal as well as possible, the timetable is drawn up by the immigrant. Only the requirement of at least 10 hours of class attendance per week is made. On which day, when and how many lessons of national language are attended in which classes is left up to the learner. Performance records are made together with the primary school students. Volunteers who can speak and write the national language well and fluently can volunteer as language partners at the

---

63§184,4 Promotion of music, sports, film, culture and the arts: BV Art.69, §246,2 Naturalisation
64§185,3 Languages

Integration Office. Language partners teach the foreigner the domestic language and in return learn the foreigner's mother tongue. They meet more or less regularly for joint activities. Once a new language of a new federal state is developed, it is also included in the primary school curriculum and offered in language classes for all nationals of the new state.

7.7.2 Integration troop

The integration troop consists of elderly humans, preferably pensioners, who have lived inland for at least 50 years. They go around the cities in honorary service in groups of two to three persons and visit immigrants who have recently moved to the city. The integration troop gets the addresses from the Integration Office. The visits are announced and can also be scheduled, but if no one is available, they simply ring the doorbell and drop an appointment card in the letterbox. The visits last 2 to 3 hours. The topic of conversation is the national past, present and future as well as the local manners, customs and virtues. The integration troop carries at least one pack of cards as equipment.

The integration troop also organises a meeting of the new neighbours. After the meeting, the integration troop goes with the immigrants to the surrounding neighbours and introduces them. Everyone receives an invitation to the city's annual immigrant festival. The integration troop organises information visits, neighbourhood meetings and the immigrant festival together with immigrants. The residential areas with the highest proportion of foreigners are visited first by the integration troop.

7.7.3 Immigrant festival

Every year, all newly arrived foreign and domestic citizens, regardless of their nationality, are invited to a city's immigrant festival. The aim is to celebrate a festival for all newcomers every year, in which the citizens of a city welcome their new fellow citizens with their culture. For this purpose, everyone brings a dish that would fill them up and that is typical of their place of origin. The first part is this eating together of domestic and foreign food. The second part is dancing to domestic and foreign music. The third part is games for children and adults, which are a suggestion to get to know each other. The three parts of eating, dancing and playing occur in every immigrant festival. Participation in this festival is voluntary.

7.7.4 Integration bus

The integration bus is offered 4 times a year, but only if at least 2 inmates are registered. Departure times are listed in the Integration Directory and are handed out as a leaflet to newcomers in a city when they register at the local Integration Office. At least one trip on the integration bus is obligatory for foreigners. Voluntary contact for a registration request is made through the People's Computer, the Internet's Integration Directory or by telephone. Registered immigrants are picked up at their front door. Anyone wishing to travel unregistered according to the timetable must come to the starting point at the Integration Office in the Town Hall. The vehicles vary in size depending on the number of registered occupants. Vehicles and crew cars of the security forces with voluntary services, for example the voluntary fire brigade, are used. This allows them to directly advertise for volunteers. The destinations are domestic and city restaurants or bars, clubs for sports, music, culture or other, honorary and charitable unifications as well as city sights. On site, the immigrants are shown what is done and how. Be it table manners in a restaurant or flirting in a bar, what is done in a club and what rights and duties members of the club have, or who helps whom on an honorary basis and why. Each bus trip is accompanied by a field staff member of the Integration Agency like a city guide on a guided tour. This staff member asks in advance about all the stops on the integration bus, puts them together, talks to the participants on the spot about what they would like to offer or say and what information is important for immigrants in any case.

7.7.5 Integration theatre

The courses for the integration theatre take place in state premises outside opening hours so that they do not have to be rented. These are, for example, schools, town halls, city halls or the like. A teacher from the drama school teaches the participants the art of improvisational theatre. Besides the usual physical exercises, acting exercises always have something to do with integration and culture. During the course, several scenes and plays are invented and developed by the participants and performed in front of the other course participants. The course decides together on interesting or funny productions and practices these productions. At the end of each course there is a staged evening on a stage in front of an audience. Whether this performance takes place in the local gymnasium, town hall or theatre is decided by the drama teacher together with the participants of his courses. There are such performances every 3 to 6 months. If not enough participants come together, positions are cancelled and one has to travel further or wait longer to be able to participate in an integration theatre. Registration for an Integration Theatre is done via the Integration Office or via the Integration Directory.

Participation in this offer is voluntary for guests and nationals, but compulsory during the naturalisation phase. The first participation in a course is free of charge, all further courses are chargeable. The costs are the salary costs of the drama teacher plus 10 % profits divided by the number of participants. The drama teacher decides how many persons can participate in a course. Priority for participation is given first to naturalised persons during their naturalisation period, then to guests or nationals.

The drama teacher has the right to dismiss participants from the course in case of bad behaviour. A refund of the money paid is not possible. In the case of guests and naturalised persons, a report will also be submitted to the responsible Integration Office and noted in the Integration Directory.

7.7.6 Civil defence lessons

Civil defence lessons are organised by each Integration Office with the local comprehensive school and the police station. Foreigners are taught social etiquette and civil defence in the comprehensive school after regular classes. Every foreigner who comes to the inland as a minor must attend these classes for at least one year between the ages of 10 and 18 and pass a final examination. Otherwise it is part of the naturalisation process.

The theoretical part of the lesson includes, for example, not spitting on the floor and, if absolutely necessary, not spitting on a sealed surface. It is better to blow your nose or spit into a handkerchief. Don't throw your own rubbish away anywhere, but keep it with you until you find a rubbish bin. Those who like to mob should use this exclusively as a means of civil courage. If you see injustice happening, you should politely point it out to the originators. What is wrong and how to politely point it out is taught in class.

The practical part is a weekly patrol at the weekend or in the evening in notorious areas for 3 months. In groups of 8 persons, the foreigners walk through the city with a backpack for rubbish and water and a rubbish tongs. They are accompanied by a patrol group from the People's Protection Service[65] . The foreigners are to practise spotting misbehaviour and drawing the attention of originators to it without provoking a fight. If there is imminent danger, the offenders may be temporarily arrested. From here on, the policeman takes over and calls for reinforcements. The policeman usually stays in the background and observes. At the end of each patrol there is feedback to all participants as well as praise and reprimands for individuals. If participants frequently show misbehaviour or a lack of willingness to participate, they can be ordered to detention in school at the police station to study the textbooks and recite what they have learned to a police officer.

The final exam is a ticking test and an assessment by the police officer. In this subject, students of different ages are together in class and in the patrol.

---

65 Ministry of Security - 6 People's Protection Service

7.8 Integration Directory

The Integration Directory serves to provide an overview of all municipalities and their different cultural orientations, corresponding offers, special immigration conditions and integration measures.

Both migrating nationals and immigrating foreigners receive a profile. Domestic nationals can participate via their profile from the Persons Directory. Refugees use their profile from the Asylum Directory.

Users can create and join groups and subgroups. Groups are established for integration measures, cultural offerings and integration committees. Sub-groups are established for individual events in the municipalities. Lawful cultural or Non-profit offers and integration measures receive a group, which is founded by the Integration Agency. In a group, users can register for the respective event.

The Integration Directory is available to nationals and naturalised persons on the intranet and to foreigners only on the internet after they have been authorised to access it. While natives have a platform for intercultural exchange and joint care of the domestic cultural heritage with the Integration Directory, immigrants have the opportunity to settle in more quickly. Foreigners must take advantage of these opportunities if they want to obtain permanent residence.

7.8.1 Admission

Admission to the Integration Directory differs depending on whether the user is a nationals, naturalised persons, guest, asylum seeker or applicant for asylum or a visa.

Admission is given to nationals via the Intranet by participating with their People's Computer. If they are immigrants from another municipality and are new to a city, they are automatically given a profile in the Integration Directory for the first 3 years. Domestic citizens can also participate in activities and discussions at any time through the Integration Directory, after all they are the ones who help newcomers to integrate or assimilate.

Naturalised persons receive admission via the intranet or the internet. Before their naturalisation, naturalised persons are guests and only receive admission via the internet. Naturalised persons have the election of whether or not they want to buy a People's Computer or regularly visit the Intranet Café to use the Intranet. If they do not wish to do so, they can continue to keep their admission via the internet. However, if they decide to do so, all data will be transferred to the intranet and the admission together with the data on the internet will be deleted.

All other foreigners living inland can only gain admission via the internet. In return, their profile is more extensive and also includes all their data from the other directories. The responsible ministries can decide whether or not the content of the data that state agencies have can also be seen on the internet. Foreigners also own the data that is collected about them. They can call up the Integration Directory in the intranet café and see their complete profile there, including all the data from all the directories, and look in an access log to see who used the data when and for what purpose.

All entries of foreigners in the Integration Directory of the Internet are transferred to the Intranet by the Ministry of Digital Affairs. The nature and extent of the admissions of foreigners to the Intranet shall be determined by the people in a committee convened by the Minister of Integration in voting with the Minister of Digital Affairs. All other conditions of access to the intranet are regulated by the Ministry of Digital Affairs.[66]

7.8.2 Profile

Anyone who wants to or has to participate in integration creates a profile of themselves in the Integration Directory. In the case of foreigners, only the Integration Agency can create the profile. Naturalised persons and nationals can create a profile themselves and copy and paste all the necessary data from the other directories. The profile of foreigners is already created before entry and contains all the data that foreigners

---

[66] Ministry of Digital Affairs - 11.3 Admission

have entered on the embassy's website and that has been recorded by state employees, such as the information from the passport or police clearance certificates. In addition, the Integration Agency adds the duration of the residence permit, whether the foreigner wants to integrate or assimilate and whether he wants to settle in the domestic country or intends to return to his home country. Depending on which identity card a foreigner receives, the Residents' Registration Office creates the status in the profile as guest or naturalised persons. Whenever state employees or honorary service providers collect data about a participant in cultural services or integration measures, this data must be entered in the Integration Directory profile. Every visit to the Integration Office and every accepted or rejected offer of state integration services is recorded in the profile. Owners of the profile have read but not write access to this information. As with all directories, users have the option to have only the information they wish to show published, with state staff having all the read rights they are authorised by law to have.

After successful naturalisation, all data of the naturalised persons are transferred to their new profile in the Persons Directory and from there entered in all directories. Asylum seekers living inland as refugees also receive a profile in the Integration Directory and add all data from the Asylum Directory there. Asylum seekers living in Asylum Villages do not need a profile because they remain among their own kind until they leave the inland again.

7.8.3 City selection

The City Selection is a programme that allows domestic and immigrant residents to find out if they are a good match for each other. With its city selection, the Integration Directory offers an overview of the cultural diversity of all domestic cities. In this way, citizens can decide for themselves when they feel that their speed of integration is no longer sufficient for a certain diversity of cultures or nations without slipping into a parallel society. On the one hand, domestic residents can try to find majorities to allow more or less cultural diversity to match their speed of integration. On the other hand, residents who are in the minority can move out and immigrate to a city that is more in line with their ideas. Immigrants are less likely to be disappointed because they are better informed in advance about their possible future home city.

7.8.3.1 Domestic characteristics

The majority preferences, interests and political views on integration among the inhabitants of a city are automatically recorded and evaluated anonymously. This evaluation is carried out automatically by an algorithm that evaluates all the information provided by the residents from all the directories and voting results and calculates an average value from this. This average value indicates the majority ratios for preferences, interests and political views.

7.8.3.2 Selection by immigrants

Immigrants can use this data of the domestic population as a guide to select or exclude possible places of residence. Once they have selected suitable locations, they can automatically search for accommodation, a job or an educational institution for their children. To do this, data access to all personal data must be enabled so that it can be automatically matched with the Real Estate Directory, the Labour Directory and the Education Directory. All remaining residences that have vacant residential properties, jobs and places in educational institutions are displayed. Users can select the most popular ones and send automatic enquiries, applications and visit the places.
In addition to this automated search function, the city selection can also be made manually and thus serves as an additional statistical overview for citizens. Especially for foreigners, the local quota of foreigners and the requirement for integration or assimilation play the biggest role. In the automated search, this information is automatically included.

7.8.3.3 Display of matching cities

In the search function for domestic cities where immigrants want to settle, there is a selection of cities on the map. You can select which cities should be highlighted on the map.

Cities in red are those where immigrants are unwanted or where the quota of foreigners has already been exhausted. Cities with a lower quota of foreigners than the national quota are coloured yellow. Clicking on the city shows what percentage of the quota has already been reached and how many persons are still allowed to move in until the quota is reached. In addition, cities are coloured yellow where assimilation is required, i.e. adaptation to the current culture without importing a foreign culture into city life. Cities in green are those in which immigrants are allowed to settle and must integrate. Integration means accepting the cultures lived in the city and being allowed to care for one's own culture in city life. Striped are cities in which only foreigners who want to leave the inland again are welcome. Dotted are cities in which only foreigners who see their new homeland inland are welcome.

For each city, immigrants can call up the percentages of nations, languages and religions in order to decide for themselves whether and which culture they still want to share with other immigrants during their life inland.

7.8.3.4 Avoidance of parallel societies

Nationals can also use these proportions as an exclusion criterion to prevent parallel societies. For example, immigrants with a certain nation or language would then no longer be allowed to immigrate if they could live a life without having to speak the national language. A parallel society is defined as a state in which all institutions of public life, such as supermarkets or physicians, are already occupied by a foreigner population group that speaks the same language and would thus establish an exclave that is merely under the same state administration. Such areas are considered social hotspots and are dissolved.[67]

---

67 Ministry of Security - 4.12 Social hotspots

7.8.4 Invitation to the integration theatre

All intranet users and users of the Integration Directory can register for courses at the Integration Theatre. If the number of participants is too low, advertising will be placed in a radius of 20km. These advertisements for an upcoming course are sent to interested users in the Integration Directory. An algorithm recognises who might be interested on the basis of the interests indicated and asks the person concerned. Those who are not interested can decline invitations and those who are interested can receive regular invitations for new courses in their area.

7.8.5 Statistics on the quota of foreigners

A database on the quota of foreigners is maintained using statistics from the Integration Agency. Users can view the domestic map on the screen and display cities, districts or the whole country via the left side panel. Now, using the many selection options, one can determine in which municipality one would like to have the quota of foreigners displayed and what percentage is already fulfilled. Whenever the search results are displayed on the map, the right side panel can be used to see how many foreigners live there and where they come from. A comment field can be used to comment on the value of the quota of foreigners displayed there with a percentage figure. For example, a quota of foreigners of 10% is displayed in a municipality. Domestic residents can comment on this value with 15% if they would like to see more foreigners, or a lower percentage if they would like to see less. Once 30% of residents have done so, a repeal quorum is triggered. In the following committee, the quota of foreigners for the municipality must be newly determined and voted on.

7.9 Departure procedures

The departure procedure regulates when and how foreigners can or must leave the country. The return policy of the Ministry of Integration includes voluntary departure, voluntary return, forced return and deportation. The Integration Agency ensures that all measures to terminate residence are initiated and enforced in cooperation with Customs.

Any nationals and foreigners may depart at any time, provided they do not do so to avoid prosecution or punishment or overstay their residence permit. Anyone who overruns his or her date of departure commits a criminal offence and is punished; the same applies to overrunning the visa period.[68]

7.9.1 Voluntary return

As soon as the nationwide quota of foreigners is exceeded, a certain number of foreigners are obliged to depart. The number is measured by the number of foreigners who exceed the quota, which is updated monthly. Accordingly, as many foreigners must depart each month until the quota of foreigners is met again. A transitional period of 3 months applies, during which foreigners can voluntarily declare their willingness to emigrate at the Integration Office. In this case, foreigners have a special right of termination to withdraw from treaties that would have a longer notice period.

To support the return, the Integration Directory offers a voting platform. The process of departure is democratically co-determined among the foreigners. The Integration Directory on the internet and intranet shows the number of persons who have to leave the domestic country. There, agreements and voting can be made on who wants to emigrate and, if necessary, to jointly deal with the departure and the new start elsewhere. If the users release their data to establish contacts, departure groups can be founded. All foreigners who want to emigrate to the same region of a country in the world are then placed in a group. As an additional function, professional qualifications can be displayed to find group members with whom a company or cooperative can be founded in the Country-of-destination.

All foreigners who are willing to depart voluntarily report to the Integration Office, which adjusts the number of necessary

---

68 Ministry of Justice - 8.9.2 Departure, 8.9.3 Expired visa, 8.18.1 Visa overstay for guest workers

departures downwards. Deportation procedures are only used if the foreigners could not agree on which of them must leave the inland and which should stay.

7.9.2 Forced return

Foreigners who need social welfare[69] because they are insolvent and inadequately insured must leave the country within 3 months. If they cannot afford the travel costs, they can go into voluntary deportation detention to work off the amount there and are then deported.

If the quota of foreigners has been exceeded and not enough foreigners report voluntarily to the integration offices for departure, certain foreigners are forced to return. Guests are forced to depart first, followed by asylum seekers, refugees and finally naturalised persons. Among the naturalised persons, naturalised persons who have children with a nationals are taken last. In general, unmated persons have to depart first, then pensioners and finally families with underage children.

The compulsion to departure consists of a personal and written request to a foreigner by field staff of the Integration Agency to leave the country within 3 months. Anyone who does not comply with the request commits a criminal offence and is put on the wanted list. After the arrest, detention pending deportation takes place. It lasts until the costs for deportation have been transferred to the Integration Agency and the deportation takes place.

7.9.3 Deportation[70]

Deportations are all departures of foreigners that are carried out under duress after a criminal offence. Those who are deported must pay the travel costs themselves in advance or work them off in a prison. In addition, contractual penalties may become due as a result of the immediate termination of all current treaties, because there is no extraordinary right

---

69 Ministry of Planned Economy - 17.1 Social welfare
70 §24,3,4,5 Protection against expulsion, extradition and deportation: BV Art.25, §243,2-6 Legislation on foreigners and asylum: BV Art. 121

of termination in the case of deportations because they are preceded by a self-inflicted criminal offence. The costs of contractual penalties must also be worked off in detention if the person to be deported cannot otherwise pay them.

The deportations take place by plane, bus, train or ship. Border crossings are monitored by Customs staff and enforced by force if necessary. The Ministry of Justice provides for sentences for offences that end in deportation.[71] The Ministry of Integration also provides for the following offences as grounds for deportation.

The deportation of individual foreigners of age of majority takes place when more than 3 offences have been legally sentenced to a fine or community service or as soon as an offence is sentenced to imprisonment. Deportation then takes place directly following detention. If the deportation costs cannot be paid, they must additionally be worked off in detention.

The deportation of an entire family consisting of both parents and their minor children takes place as soon as a minor child of the family becomes a criminal. The delinquency of the child is independent of age and is considered to have been reached when more than 5 criminal offences would be sentenced to a fine or community service or as soon as an offence would be sentenced to imprisonment. Adult criminal law is applied when determining the sentence. The age of criminal responsibility does not protect against this family deportation. Parents and siblings are automatically held jointly responsible for the failed parenting, which must not be at the expense of the domestic population. Families deported because their child is a criminal must pay the costs of proceedings, monetary fines and deportation costs. An imprisonment must be served by a deputy parent. The deportation of the rest of the family takes place immediately.

Criminal asylum seekers and refugees are immediately deported to their unsafe countries of origin. Foreigners deported for criminal offences are banned from entering the domestic territory for life. Whoever disregards the entry ban

---

71 Ministry of Justice - 8.9.4 Deportations

commits a criminal offence.[72]

7.9.4 Readmission

The departure of foreigners from the inland and their entry into their country of origin must in principle be possible, otherwise nationals of that foreign country may not enter at all. If this agreement is not adhered to by other states, the Ministry of Foreign Affairs enters into negotiations with the responsible ministry of the state through its embassy. In the negotiations, various punitive measures are offered, ranging from entry bans for all nationals of the affected state, to trade bans, to the severance of all economic and diplomatic relations. Negotiations on readmission are conducted by the Ministry of Foreign Affairs in cooperation with the indoor service of the Integration Agency.

Deportations are usually communicated to the Country-of-destination through the embassy in the country and accompanied to the border by customs officers. If the countries refuse to accept the refugees despite negotiated punitive measures, there are two options.

The first option is a clandestine transfer of the deportees to their country of origin. The border violation is to be as small as possible, but still ensure that the deported foreigners arrive in their country of origin. Deportees are placed in a container and flown by plane to the border of the Country-of-destination. The container is dropped by a flying drone that carries the container. The deportees are placed in this container, which keeps the pressure, heat and oxygen at a humanly healthy level. Above the container are four parachutes that allow the container to sink stably to the ground. Underneath the container, a cushion of air inflates after the drop, ensuring a soft landing. Breathing air in the container for all occupants is ensured via an air shaft. After the doors of the containers have been closed from the outside, they can also be opened from the inside after the drop. In the case of a border with the ocean, the container can also be brought underwater to the coast by a drone so that the deportees can disembark there.

72Ministry of Justice - 8.9.5 Failure to comply with the entry ban

The second option is used if an act of war is suspected for the first option. It consists of detaining the deportees until the entry permit is granted or the deportees carry out their departure independently and are escorted by Customs to the border.

7.9.5 Lack of nationality

Foreigners without passports cannot enter the country. If they have nevertheless done so, they are guilty of illegal entry and will be deported. They must declare where they were born and what nationality their parents have. Anyone who refuses to provide the information or can be shown to have falsified it is committing a criminal offence punishable by one year's detention. To identify or verify them, a genetic test is taken that locates where they came from. Through automated speech recognition, voice samples of the foreigner are taken and compared with a database. A biometric passport photo is also taken of the foreigner, which is sent to the embassies in the affected states along with all the personal data collected. Affected states are all states that are eligible through the genetic test and the language sample. The embassies, in cooperation with local authorities, try to find similarities to persons holding a passport of that country on the basis of the photo and its biometric data. This means that a data comparison must be made with the biometric data of the photo and the archives of the affected country to find out whether there was already a passport for this citizen in that country. Countries that do not want to agree to this will be threatened with penalties in negotiations. The readmission procedure is applied accordingly.

8 Asylum[73]

Asylum law covers all areas of the asylum procedure, from asylum applicant to departure. During the asylum procedure, asylum seekers can decide to become refugees or to remain asylum seekers. Refugee law regulates the naturalisation procedure for refugees.

The law on freedom of movement stipulates that asylum seekers are not allowed to settle freely inland, but are initially accommodated in Social Villages and then in Asylum Villages. If asylum seekers want to leave these places, they receive a temporary travel permit, which is noted on their identity card. The travel permit can be restricted locally if municipalities or neighbouring states do not want asylum seekers to enter.

The right of residence stipulates that the residence permits of asylum seekers and refugees are linked to the security of their country of origin. As soon as the country of origin is safe again, the residence permit ends.

The Hardship Commission is responsible for making a decision in borderline cases. The Hardship Commission is a municipal or national asylum committee. It decides whether an asylum seeker may still decide to become a refugee after moving to an Asylum Village or whether asylum seekers must first finish building the Asylum Village before they leave, or whether refugees who are about to be naturalised must also return to their country of origin. The Hardship Commission meets when an appropriate veto quorum is met.

8.1 Asylum Committee

In the Asylum Committee, questions are clarified as to what grounds for asylum are and whether the people's position is in accordance with international law. Overall, it is about when and why someone is granted asylum, what asylum looks like inland and what conditions apply to immigration. The Asylum Committee is convened by the Minister of Integration as soon as the asylum law is to be changed, so that all affected citizens and ministries can participate.

73§243.1 Legislation on foreigners and asylum: BV Art. 121, §244.4 Management of immigration

8.2 Reception capacities

The reception capacity is influenced by various capacity limits. The indoor service of the Integration Agency is responsible for collecting and compiling the necessary data and forwarding it to the responsible agencies. In the first place, there is the national quota of foreigners, which may not be exceeded. In second place are the municipal quotas of foreign nationals, which may not be exceeded by refugees. Also decisive are the citizens' decisions after voting on whether an Asylum Village may be built in the neighbourhood of the municipality. In third place are the capacities in the initial reception facilities of the Social Villages. In fourth place are the structural limits of the Asylum Villages and in fifth place the voluntary host families for refugees.

The indoor service informs the embassies, via their quotas, how many asylum application procedures[74] they may open. Since asylum seekers in the Social Villages and the Asylum Villages speak the same language and, if possible, have the same nationality, the capacity limits of the Social Villages and the Asylum Villages decide which embassy may accept or reject asylum application procedures. The capacities of the Asylum Villages and host families decide how many asylum applications may be granted. The capacities in the Social Villages decide on the dates of entry.

All accommodation facilities report their capacities of sleeping places to the indoor service and all embassies report all approved asylum applications to it. The indoor service ensures an automated allocation of asylum seekers at full capacity from the embassies via the Social Villages and the Asylum Village or host family. If there is insufficient capacity in the Social Villages, waiting lists are drawn up. If there is insufficient capacity in the Asylum Villages for one language, the asylum application procedures in countries with that language are suspended. When the quota of foreigners nationwide is reached, all asylum application procedures are suspended. Asylum applicants can join a waiting list or apply for asylum in another country.

The capacity of host families depends on how many nationals

74 Ministry of Foreign Affairs - 9 Asylum application procedures

and naturalised persons are willing to host refugees. Refugees and host families are placed by the Asylum Directory. Unwanted refugees who are rejected by their host family or who have not found one at all have to move to the Asylum Village.

The reception capacity of an Asylum Village depends on how many accommodation facilities can be created. The housebuilding programme, with its 9 000 containers for 6 persons each and 1000 supply containers, creates space and work for 54 000 asylum seekers in total. All these asylum seekers are used for house building and can produce housing units for a maximum of 60 000 inhabitants within one year. As soon as houses are ready for occupancy, the asylum seekers move out of the containers into the houses and new asylum seekers can follow from the Social Villages. Provided there is no rush, houses can also be built more slowly and to a higher standard. The fastest option is only chosen if the people want to exhaust their quota of foreigners as quickly as possible and need many new housing units in at least one city.

8.3 Asylum Directory

In the Asylum Directory, asylum seekers have a profile and can change it to a refugee profile and vice versa. The change is only possible once. Refugees can move to the Asylum Village at any time, but cannot move back. Refugees transfer their profile to the Integration Directory when they start their naturalisation. For domestic families, Residential Communities or companies that are willing to host refugees, there is a group for host families. There they can choose the refugees they want to host until the refugees are naturalised. Refugees can choose domestic families, Residential Communities or companies to live and work with in the Host Family Group until they are naturalised. Refugees can mark their profile as "available" again if they would like to change host families. Each individual host family automatically opens a subgroup where they introduce themselves and exchange information with applicants.

With its establishment, each Asylum Village automatically receives a group. There, asylum seekers can choose Asylum

Villages and see in which Asylum Village their language is spoken, their religious group is represented and where fellow citizens from their region of origin already live. If there are several villages, they can choose their favourite location from all the locations with available capacity. All asylum seekers in an asylum village group can organise themselves there together in order to set up companies in their home country after their return, to form working communities or to recruit asylum seekers and refugees from their country of origin as employees or investors. For individual projects, sub-groups can be formed in which members can exchange information and write news. The asylum village groups and their functions are modelled on the Social Directory .[75]

8.3.1 Asylum Directory website

The access data for this website is given to the asylum seeker after the asylum application has been approved. There you can add to your profile in the Asylum Directory already created by the embassy. You should state what you can do and what you like. In addition, you can express wishes as to what your host family should be like or in which Asylum Village you will end up. If relatives or acquaintances are already inland, this family may also be mentioned specifically. The names and dates of birth of the persons affected are necessary for this.

All entries are written in the national language of the asylum seekers, because ready-made selection options are translated into all languages of unsafe countries of origin. Free text fields have to be translated by the profile holders themselves. The file is now stored in an intranet folder at the embassy. The data is transmitted in encrypted form via the Internet and placed in the Asylum Directory by the Ministry of Digital Affairs. In the Social Village, the asylum seekers and refugees can access their profiles again.

In the first step, asylum seekers choose their language. The page content is then displayed in this language. In the second step, the first reception centre is found. To do this, one enters a country of origin, the last place of residence there and the

75 Ministry of Planned Economy - 4.6 Social Directory

religious affiliation. Then the appropriate Social Village is automatically displayed. If there are several Social Villages, all places on the displayed map are to be rated in a ranking order. In the allocation process, the wishes are taken into account as far as the Social Village's admission capacity allows. In the third step, users decide whether they want to become an asylum seeker or a refugee. Asylum seekers choose the Asylum Village where their culture predominates. If there are several, all villages on the displayed map are to be ranked. In the allocation process, wishes are taken into account as far as the reception capacity of an Asylum Village allows. Refugees choose the host families they would like to move in with and work with. The host family then contacts them to get to know them and meet them at the initial reception centre.

All data from the internet version of the Asylum Directory is regularly transferred to the intranet version and vice versa. The Ministry of Digital Affairs is responsible for the transfer of the data.

8.3.2 Views

Asylum Directory Profile	**Refugee** icon (running stick figure)
[Profile picture]	First name, last name, date of birth
[Partner & Children]	Marital status (single, partnered, number of children)
	Training (select from list)
	Professional experience (select from list)
	Place of origin (select from world map) Passions (sport, religion, gay, etc)

Asylum Directory Subgroup	**Host family** icon (house with 4 stick figures)
[Profile picture]	Family name, place of residence, maximum persons capacity
[Person 1]	Name, age, profession
[Person 2]	Name, age, profession
[...]	If applicable, more persons in the family

Asylum Directory Subgroup	**Family business** icon (factory with 4 stick figures)
[Profile picture]	Family name, place of residence, maximum persons capacity
[Person 1]	Name, age, profession
[Person 2]	Name, age, profession
[...]	If applicable, more persons in the family business
[vacancy]	Activity, number of hours per week, working hours, product/service

Asylum Directory Profile	**Asylum seeker** icon (running stick figure with backpack)
[Profile picture]	First name, last name, date of birth
[Partner & Children]	Marital status (single, partnered, number of children) Link to the profiles of the family members
	Training (select from list)
	Professional experience (select from list)
	Place of origin (select from world map) Passions (sport, religion, gay, etc)

Asylum Directory Group	**Asylum Village** icon (4 houses)
[Aerial photo]	Location, population, maximum capacity
[Culture]	Language spoken, religion practised, country/countries of origin
[vacancies]	In shops or businesses of the other asylum seekers
[liberal professions]	Appeals that do not yet exist in this Asylum Village, but are necessary.

8.4 Asylum procedure

In the asylum procedure, the Integration Agency's field service accompanies asylum seekers from entry to departure. All formalities, motions and concerns can be dealt with or enquired about by asylum seekers or those looking after them at the Integration Office. While the accommodation of asylum applicants is still carried out independently abroad, the final allocation of residence for asylum villages or host families is carried out in the follow-up accommodation in the Social Village. The Integration Agency is responsible for management and statistics. The People's Protection Service is responsible for the security in the Asylum Villages and the Customs is responsible for deportations. The aim of the asylum seeker procedure is to prepare asylum seekers with the same refugee background for the tasks that lie ahead when they return home. For some this will be building a house in a destroyed city, for others it will be building up parties and press organs.

8.4.1 Financing

In order to finance the asylum procedure, the Ministry of Integration provides advance financing and the asylum seekers pay the costs. The entire financial process is handled by the People's Bank. The entire asylum procedure is pre-financed by the Ministry of Integration, so that flight tickets and building materials are already paid for. As soon as the asylum seekers transfer their assets, they replace the pre-financing. The embassies are instructed to accept the richest asylum applicants first in order to provide start-up funding for poorer asylum applicants later on.

During their stay in the Asylum Village, asylum seekers live according to the rules of Planned Economy, with luxury supply being replaced by house building. The Asylum Villages are thus largely self-financing. The conversion of Asylum Villages into new neighbourhoods after all asylum seekers have moved out and the sale of all real estate enables the repayment of assets to the asylum seekers. Travel and accommodation costs are deducted from this. 5% interest is paid after completion of an Asylum Village. Surpluses of up to 10% go to the Ministry of Integration, the rest to the state treasury. The respective host family is responsible for financing refugees. Once refugees are naturalised, they finance themselves.

8.4.1.1 Asset management

Asylum seekers automatically receive an account with the People's Bank with their approved asylum application. Asylum seekers must pay all their financial assets into this account shortly before their departure and close all other accounts. The closure of the accounts is checked by an automated query at all possible banks in the world. Asylum seekers are only allowed to have one account with the People's Bank, no other. Refugees are only allowed to open an account with another bank once they are naturalised.

Asylum seekers must turn all their assets into money as far as possible in order to be able to transport them. All financial products such as shares, bonds, derivatives, precious metals and currency reserves must be sold. If possible, valuables such as real estate or furnishings can be stored or rented out during the absence in the country of origin. Revenues from these assets and any financial assets must be deposited in an account with the People's Bank before entering the domestic country. The amount is exchanged into the currency of Social Market Economy[76] at the current exchange rate, because countries of origin tend to have devaluing currencies. If a bank transfer is not possible for security reasons, asylum seekers can also bring their money in cash to an embassy where they have gone through the asylum application procedure. This embassy then exchanges the money and makes the entry in the account at the People's Bank. Already when filling out the asylum application, the amount is asked for, which may later vary by 10% when the money is actually transferred.

Asylum seekers can only access their financial assets again when they leave the inland. This also includes asylum seekers who are deported for criminal offences, whereby compensation payments and monetary fines are deducted. The assets of all asylum seekers are thus probably higher overall than at the time of entry and have not suffered losses in the value of the currency of the country of origin.

76Ministry of Social Market Economy - 13.1 National currency of the Social Market Economy

8.4.1.2 People's Bank online account

The People's Bank account provides online access for each asylum seeker to view their account balances and check deposits into that account. The home page shows the total assets in all necessary currencies. Asylum seekers can see their deposited assets in the currency of their country of origin at the daily exchange rate into the national currency of the Social Market Economy, the amount in the national currency of the Social Market Economy and their working hours in the Social Village or Asylum Village. At the People's Bank branch in the Asylum Village Security Centre, asylum seekers administer their accounts at ATMs in their national language.

The currency of their country of origin is familiar to the asylum seekers and they are better able to calculate in these monetary units because they know the prices of products. Therefore, the amount in the national currency of the Social Market Economy is converted into the currency of their country of origin on a daily basis. Depending on whether the value of the currency from the country of origin decreases or increases, the account balance in foreign currency increases or decreases because the assets are invested in the national currency of the Social Market Economy. In addition, all asylum seekers from the same country can see their joint account balance, but not the account balances of each individual. This overview can only be displayed if an asylum seeker allows other asylum seekers to view his account balance. This makes it easier to set up cooperatives and companies in the country of origin.

The amount in national currency remains the same unless additions or debits are made. After the initial deposit of the total assets, further deposits are only possible if an asylum seeker has an ongoing income, for example through licences or the renting of own real estate. Debits may only be made by the Integration Agency in order to settle travel expenses or wage costs of domestic professionals in care facilities in the Asylum Villages. If an asylum seeker's financial assets are not sufficient to cover the costs he or she incurs, he or she must work off the amount in arrears before departure in detention.

8.4.1.3 Asylum Village real estate bonds

The remaining amount, minus all costs, is invested entirely in People's Bank real estate bonds, the term of which is linked to the asylum seeker's stay inland. The interest rate is 5% per completed Asylum Village. Refugees get their money back as soon as they are naturalised, but without interest because they have not done any construction work.

The assets of all asylum seekers thus flow into the real estate fund to buy building materials for the houses in the Asylum Villages. The Ministry of Infrastructure takes care of the construction machinery and experts and is reimbursed for its costs after the houses are sold. The finished houses are sold to nationals and naturalised persons at 15% profits above the construction costs. For all nationals, the People's Bank offers a hire-purchase scheme financed by property bonds on the People's Stock Exchange. As soon as the asylum seekers move out of the Asylum Village, the new owners move into and pay for their houses.

The asylum seekers receive their money back directly before departure, including interest and less costs incurred, including return travel costs. Asylum seekers are shown how much money all asylum seekers have paid in, i.e. how big the real estate fund is, when they look at their account balances. A horizontal bar chart shows the number of houses built with the money. When the bar is full, the Asylum Village is completed and 5% interest is paid on each asylum seeker's funds. If the asylum seekers move and build another Asylum Village, the bar starts again. This is to make it clear to the asylum seekers that they can get richer faster together if they also invest their assets in joint projects later in their country of origin.

8.4.1.4 Cryptocurrency

During their stay inland, the asylum seekers have no access to their assets because they are entirely invested in real estate bonds for the Asylum Villages. The asylum seekers do not need money inland because they live according to the rules of Planned Economy and only a cryptocurrency[77] is necessary for this. Throughout their stay inland, the asylum seekers use either the Social Card[78] in the Social Village or their Asylum ID Card in the Asylum Village as a means of payment. The asylum ID card additionally receives all the functions of the social card and serves as a bank card for the People's Bank. All work performed by an asylum seeker in the Asylum Village is settled via the asylum ID and can be viewed as an account balance. The currency working hours from the Planned Economy is also used in the Asylum Villages. However, trade with Social Villages is not possible, only trade with other Asylum Villages. All services that asylum seekers access in the welfare villages are debited from the working hours account.

8.4.2 Responsibilities[79]

The Ministry of Integration regulates the basic issues of asylum policy in voting with the Ministries of Foreign Affairs, Security, Planned Economy and Infrastructure. With its quota of foreigners, the Ministry of Integration specifies the maximum number of asylum seekers that may be allowed into the country until the nationwide quota of foreigners is exhausted. The Ministry of Foreign Affairs is responsible for determining safe and unsafe countries of origin[80] and handles the entire asylum application procedure[81] through its embassies. It ensures that asylum applications are not submitted more than once by sharing data with other Continental Union member states. The Ministry of Security is responsible for entry and departure as well as security in Asylum Villages.[82] The Ministry of Planned Economy is responsible for initial reception after crossing the border.[83] After that, the Ministry of Integration is responsible for the distribution of refugees

---

77 Ministry of Planned Economy - 13.2 Digital currency Working hours
78 Ministry of Planned Economy - 4.7 Social card
79 §243.1 Legislation on foreigners and asylum: BV Art. 121, §244.4 Management of immigration
80 Ministry of Foreign Affairs - 9.1 Unsafe countries of origin
81 Ministry of Foreign Affairs - 9 Asylum application procedures
82 Ministry of Security - 8 Customs, 6 People's Protection Service
83 Ministry of Planned Economy - 18.5 Asylum

in host families and the accommodation of asylum seekers in the Asylum Village and the social services there. The Ministry of Integration, together with the Ministry of Infrastructure, manages the construction of houses in the Asylum Villages.[84]

8.4.3 Asylum application

Asylum applicants apply for asylum at an embassy where the language of the asylum applicant is spoken.[85] If it is too dangerous to visit the embassy in their country of origin, they can go to an embassy in a neighbouring country.

Embassies serve asylum applicants worldwide as safe travel agencies without fear of being pursued by secret services or the police of the refugee country. The aim is for asylum seekers to make a safe escape without smugglers and robbers and to know that they can book this escape like a trip at a travel agency. In this way, a wave of refugees can be processed like a wave of travellers at holiday time.

Asylum is to be granted to humans who are threatened with death in their home country, whether through persecution or war. The Ministry of Foreign Affairs determines which countries of origin are considered unsafe. Another prerequisite is that asylum seekers have not committed a criminal offence under domestic law or have already applied for asylum in another country. For this purpose, the embassies have Customs check the asylum seeker's data against the database for criminal offences and asylum applications.

If the asylum application is approved, a profile is created in the Asylum Directory and a travel date is set, which depends on the waiting list. The waiting list monitors the capacity of the asylum houses in the Social Villages. The Ministry of Foreign Affairs is responsible until entry and hands the asylum seekers the approved asylum application, which entitles them to entry.

---

84 Ministry of Infrastructure - 5.13 Housebuilding programme
85 Ministry of Foreign Affairs - 9.2 Asylum application in embassies

8.4.4 Entry of asylum seekers

Typically, asylum seekers enter from their country of origin or a safe neighbouring country by scheduled flight, charter flight, military aircraft, private shipping company ship or navy. The means of transport chosen depends on the number of asylum seekers from a country of origin and the most cost-effective option. Accordingly, clearance takes place at the domestic border posts at the airport or seaport. If asylum seekers wish to travel themselves, they must select a border post for their entry.

The Ministry of Foreign Affairs ensures that the asylum seekers are brought inland. They are allowed to take 20 kilograms of luggage per person. All transport costs are initially borne by the Ministry of Foreign Affairs and charged to the asylum seekers. Payment must be made as soon as the asylum application has been approved or, in case of financial hardship, before departure after the asylum stay. If the asylum seeker is unable to pay by then, the money must be developed in detention.

Asylum seekers must report to Customs at the nearest border post as soon as they set foot on domestic soil.[86] There, the asylum seeker is classified as "entered" in the Travel Directory. Customs then reports the entry to the responsible Embassy and Integration Office in the designated Social Village. The data of the asylum application is compared with the passport, fingerprints and iris and cross-checked with the data recorded at the embassy and newly with the continental database for criminal offences and asylum applications. Criminal asylum seekers are not allowed into the country and lose their asylum status. If they cannot leave the country themselves, they are deported. All other asylum seekers are picked up by People's Protection Service vehicles at the border post and taken to their designated Social Village.

86Ministry of Security - 8.2.5 Entry of foreigners

8.4.5 Initial recording

The initial reception of asylum seekers takes place for 6 months in the Social Villages.[87] Only one foreign language may be spoken in a Social Village and asylum seekers may not make up more than 10% of the inhabitants of a Social Village. Accordingly, all asylum seekers are distributed among all Social Villages in the country. Occupancy is already booked for each asylum seeker by the embassy, so that long transport routes between the border post and the Social Village are avoided.

Upon entry into the Social Village, asylum seekers receive the social card at the gate, which they use to settle all benefits in the Social Village and to identify themselves. At the Residents' Registration Office of the Social Village they receive their asylum ID.

Basically, all neighbours help the new arrivals with the move. Accordingly, all asylum house residents help each other with moving in and out and are welcomed and supported by their sponsors.[88]

All asylum seekers are accommodated in the asylum house and take on work in basic supply. In theoretical and practical lessons, they learn all Planned Economy techniques of basic supply and house construction as well as domestic criminal law, state organisation law and asylum law. The aim of these shortened lessons is to enable asylum seekers to run their future Asylum Village in a Planned Economy as independently as possible. The training centres find out which qualifications are needed in the Asylum Village and train voluntary asylum seekers to become the appropriate skilled workers. Since all asylum seekers in a Social Village speak the same language, they will also move to the same Asylum Village. This is to promote friendships among the asylum seekers who will support each other after their return.

Since the residents of an Asylum Village come from the same region or country if possible, but may enter at different times, moves between Asylum Villages may become necessary. In principle, each Asylum Village is supported with asylum seekers from the initial reception until the capacity limit is

---

87 Ministry of Planned Economy - 18.5 Asylum
88 Ministry of Planned Economy - 18.5.2 Sponsors

reached.

From the first week after moving in, every asylum seeker who wants to become a refugee can change his or her profile in the Asylum Directory in the Social Village Intranet Café. This is about asylum seekers deciding whether they want to stay inland and thus become a refugee or whether they want to return home as soon as their country of origin is safe again and thus remain an asylum seeker. The decision whether to remain an asylum seeker or become a refugee must be made after 4 months at the latest.

As soon as a refugee has found a place of accommodation in a family, Residential Community or company that finances his or her life, the Social Service in cooperation with the host family arranges the move. Refugees are not obliged to stay in the Social Village for 6 months.

8.5 Refugees

Refugees are asylum seekers who want to settle inland and have submitted a motions for naturalisation in the Integration Directory. Asylum seekers only become refugees when they leave the Social Village and move in with a host family. Refugees who have not found a host family after 6 months must move to the Asylum Village, but may continue to search for a host family in the Asylum Directory.

Once they are accepted into a host family, they receive lessons in the national language for a maximum of 6 months. Those who do not pass the final test of a course must repeat the course as often as necessary until they pass. In order to be naturalised, further performance records over a longer period of time are necessary. Refugees take the naturalisation test during their stay with host families. If they pass it, they can begin the naturalisation phase. To meet all the requirements, they must, among other things, move out of the host family, find work and be able to live independently.

8.5.1 Host family

Any nationals and naturalised persons may take in refugees and become their guardians until a refugee is naturalised. The guardian has the duty to support his refugee with all the necessities of life and has the right to make the refugee work for it. Any money earned by a refugee must be transferred to the guardian's account. The guardian does not receive any money from the state.

While refugees are living in the Social Village, the potential host families come to visit and decide whether and which refugee suits them. The refugees also decide during the visit whether the host family suits them. The refugee and the host family must accept or reject the host family within 7 days by submitting a report in the Asylum Directory to the Integration Agency. As soon as the asylum status expires, but at the earliest after 5 years, the refugees must be naturalised. After passing naturalisation, refugees are considered naturalised and only have to return to their country of origin if they become criminals or insolvent.

Refugees are not allowed to switch freely between the four economic forms. They are bound to their host families, in case of doubt to the guardian. Refugees are only allowed to work in the families, Residential Communities and family businesses of the Social Market Economy and Free Market Economy where they live.

If the refugee has indicated a specific host family in the Asylum application or Asylum Directory, the guardian with a valid domestic identity card must pick up the refugee from the Social Village. The address given by the refugee must be indicated on the identity card of the guardian picking up the refugee from the host family.

In case of unemployment, a refugee must move to the Asylum Village if the guardian can no longer or no longer wants to support him or her. When the country of origin becomes safe again, all refugees are deported, regardless of whether they live in the Asylum Village or with a host family. Refugees are naturalised after 5 years at the earliest and are only deported if they are criminals, after they have served their imprisonment.

8.6 Asylum seekers

Asylum seekers want to return to their country of origin. Therefore, they hardly have to learn the national language and do not have to display domestic virtues or adopt the domestic culture. For them, a social copy of their home country is created in their self-built Asylum Village, although the criminal law and the democratic order of the inland apply. Asylum seekers prepare their successful return in the Asylum Village. As soon as their country of origin is safe again, they leave the Asylum Village within 3 months.

8.6.1 Asylum Village

The purpose of the Asylum Villages is, on the one hand, to provide accommodation and further education for asylum seekers and, on the other hand, to create new housing for the domestic population. The asylum seekers build the new houses and live in them until the entire construction project is completed. This service of solidarity by the asylum seekers creates acceptance among the population. The labour that goes into the newly built homes is the return for saving lives in times of crisis. Nationals help asylum seekers by lending them shelter and farmland. Asylum seekers help nationals by building them houses.

The municipalities report to the Integration Agency when new residential areas are to be developed. In return, they submit a development plan and win over buyers in advance who can have their future houses built according to their ideas.

8.6.1.1 Move

After the 6 months in the Social Village, all the asylum seekers move into the common new Asylum Village, which initially consists only of containers and building materials. Based on the data from their profiles, asylum seekers with suitable vocational training are assigned to the appropriate positions in basic supply and house construction. The Social Service carries out the moves and sets up a mobile Social Village[89] together with the asylum seekers. All the asylum seekers move in there one by one until all the utilities and living containers are in place. Then the construction of the houses begins. First, the cheapest prefabricated housing units are built. Asylum seekers from the mobile Social Village gradually move into these housing units. At the end, the highest-quality housing units are built, in which asylum seekers no longer move in because the low-cost housing units are sufficient for their accommodation. Once all the asylum seekers have moved out of the mobile Social Village, it is dismantled and taken to the next building site. There, the asylum seekers rebuild it and build a new Asylum Village.

8.6.1.2 Utilities

The utilities of the mobile Social Village will be placed to cover vacancies in the development plan that will be closed after the withdrawal, such as roads or public squares and parks. Utilities include a commercial kitchen, laundry, infirmary, school, showers and toilets, and a biogas plant. A factory for building materials, components and prefabricated houses is being built on the outskirts of the Asylum Village. All asylum seekers who do not work on the construction sites work in the factories. The asylum seekers are supposed to go through all areas of real estate production and basic supply as far as possible.

8.6.1.3 Compulsory education

The school-age children of asylum seekers are taught in their national language by asylum seekers who are trained teachers. If there are not enough teachers among the asylum seekers, voluntary asylum seekers with the most suitable training possible have to take over the teaching. These voluntary teachers are supported by Virtual Reality glasses[90] with

---

89 Ministry of Planned Economy - 19 Mobile Social Villages
90 Ministry of Digital Affairs - 13.6.9.1 Virtual reality glasses

instructions and teaching materials in their national language. The school children receive practical housekeeping lessons in the afternoons while working in the large kitchen, the laundry and the cleaning and waste disposal of the Asylum Village. In the last two school years, the children go through the prefabricated house building process, from production in the factory, to installation on the construction site, to interior finishing.

8.6.1.4 Community

All asylum seekers in an Asylum Village are to become friends who help each other build their houses after their return. Building communities are founded for this purpose. Building communities are asylum seekers who get along well with each other and come from similar regions in their homeland. In the Asylum Village, manners, customs and religions may be lived out very freely, as long as international human rights are respected and domestic criminal law is not violated. Two asylum seekers always accompany the patrol of the People's Protection Service.

8.6.1.5 House building

The Asylum Village is being built through the housebuilding programme of the Ministry of Infrastructure. For this purpose, the Ministry of Infrastructure provides mobile factories for building materials, components and prefabricated houses in containers, as well as building materials, construction machinery and skilled personnel as part of the construction team from the housebuilding programme.[91] Skilled personnel are only provided to the extent that they are not available in the mass of asylum seekers. All construction workers receive training at the Education Centre on what the construction plans look like. Each asylum seeker decides on a job with the help of the duty roster of the Planned Economy[92] and has to learn the theory by distance learning if he does not know it

91 Ministry of Infrastructure - 5.8 Construction Team, 5.13 Housebuilding programme
92 Ministry of Planned Economy - 7.6 Duty roster

yet. For this purpose, the respective training courses from the educational system of the prisons[93] are translated into the respective national language of the country of origin.

The asylum seekers are divided into construction workers, construction supervisors and architects. Senior architects of the Construction Team constantly monitor all progress. The construction sites are video-monitored so that it is automatically recognised when faults occur on the construction site and the site manager is automatically alerted. He is shown the error view on his Virtual Reality glasses and can use loudspeakers to prevent the affected construction worker from continuing work in order to avoid subsequent errors. The images from the video surveillance are compared with the digital construction plan by a computer programme. The digital construction plan is created by cameras recording the sample construction once and comparing it with all subsequent identical constructions. If repeated or deliberate faults are found during construction, the asylum seeker is demoted back to construction worker. Construction workers who make more than 3 faults must work in the building materials and components factory. Those who make too many faults there as well must work in the utilities.

8.6.1.6 Development plan

The development plan is specified by the municipality and the building style is specified by the subsequent owners. All other flats and houses are built in different construction forms and styles. The building forms are detached houses, terraced houses and apartment buildings with balconies, gardens and halls that can be used as garages, barns or business premises. Building styles include prefabricated houses, timber houses, mud houses, half-timbered houses and buildings made of concrete and steel. All houses are energy efficient and as energy self-sufficient as possible. Prefabricated house producers produce training videos that are translated and create a list of their production machines. The best production machines are ordered in multiples and used in the mobile factories.

---

93 Ministry of Justice - 7.5.11.1 Training

The building material corresponds to what is most available in the soil at the building site. Since the soil in the asylum seekers' country of origin may be different, different methods of construction are taught. At least one house must be built in the practical lessons with the building materials adapted to the soil conditions of the country of origin. In this way, the asylum seekers can practise how to build their own houses in their homeland after their stay inland. Asylum seekers who can build domestic houses according to their cultural building style should build at least one such example in the Asylum Village, which will be listed as a monument to the builders of the Asylum Village.

8.6.1.7 Owner

Later house owners can already submit their building plans and have a say in how their house should be built and can commission their own architects. If possible, the future homeowners should already help with the construction work and thus get to know the asylum seekers who are building it.

8.6.1.8 Completion

Once an Asylum Village is built, the containers move to the next location, where a residential area is to be built on the orders of a municipality. If more asylum seekers arrive with the same language, a new Asylum Village is built by the new arrivals. If no more asylum seekers arrive, the asylum seekers move out of the completed Asylum Village and build another one at a different location. In this case, the asylum seekers receive a further 5% interest on their invested assets and the new house owners can move in immediately and pay off their house in a hire-purchase scheme. All houses must be sold when the asylum seekers depart so that their assets can be paid out to them including the interest. For nationals, the People's Bank offers loans so that they can continue to use the hire-purchase scheme.

8.6.1.9 Reintegration of asylum seekers

Asylum seekers are specially trained in the Asylum Villages to take up the necessary reconstruction work in their country of origin immediately after their return. For this purpose, work groups are already formed in the Asylum Village, which are specialised in different industries and fields of work and have enjoyed corresponding lessons in the Asylum Village. The skills taught are adapted to the causes of flight.

House building, home economics and business management are the most important things asylum seekers must be able to do when they return to their devastated homeland. Returning asylum seekers are offered a cheap loan to buy the manufacturing machinery for prefabricated house production, which they already know how to use.

The assets of all asylum seekers from the same country or region are held in an Asylum Village. Asylum seekers are supposed to form economic partnerships in the Asylum Village and pool parts of their savings to collect start-up capital. This should then be used to set up cooperatives, houses or companies in the country of origin, which the asylum seekers have thought up together during their time in the Asylum Village and, if possible, have already tried out. Events are held in the Asylum Village to present business ideas and find business partners. Asylum seekers can profitably implement these contacts in their home country after their return.

8.6.1.10 Domestic economy

When there are no more construction projects in municipalities, the asylum seekers settle down and start building a domestic economy. In the Asylum Village, the currency is Planned Economy. The background to this is that goods imported into the Asylum Village must be purchased in bundles from the cheapest supplier. The longer the asylum seekers cannot return to their unsafe country of origin, the more similar Asylum Villages become to Social Villages.

8.6.1.11 Professionals

All professionals needed for basic supply should be asylum seekers. If necessary, a specialist must do service in another Asylum Village, even if he or she does not speak the language there. These professionals work in rotation so that individual asylum seekers are never disadvantaged just because they are professionals. If domestic professionals have to be employed, the wage costs are deducted from the total assets of the asylum seekers in the Asylum Village. If there are voluntary domestic skilled workers who live and are fed in the Asylum Village but work without pay, this is honorary service.

8.6.1.12 Foreign trade

As in the Social Village, it is possible for nationals to shop in the Asylum Village. The taxes are only 20% higher. This brings the Asylum Village foreign currency, i.e. foreign currency in the national currency of the Social Market Economy, or Dollars, which can be used to finance imports. The sale of surplus production is regulated as in the Planned Economy.[94]

8.6.1.13 Cultural bazaar

The Cultural bazaar is a festival that is celebrated 2 times a year in each Asylum Village and welcomes guests from the surrounding area, like an open day. Traditional food of the asylum seekers is sold, music is played and dancing takes place. The bazaar of cultures can also give rise to new business ideas, as is common in the age of the culture industry.

8.7 Departure

As soon as a country of origin is safe again, the current Asylum Village is completed and the departure of all asylum seekers is organised. The departure of asylum seekers is not self-determined and is therefore called deportation. Travel costs

---

94Ministry of Planned Economy - 15 Foreign trade

are already paid at the time of deportation. On the day of their departure, asylum seekers are given the opportunity to transfer their assets from their account at the People's Bank to any other bank in the world. If asylum seekers do not wish to return to their country of origin, they must organise this departure themselves from their country of origin.

8.8 Punitive measures

The entire asylum procedure includes punitive measures that can limit or exclude the right to asylum. Deportations take place to the unsafe country of origin or to a country willing to take in criminal asylum seekers. The asylum seekers then receive their assets back without interest and with costs deducted. If the assets are not sufficient to pay the return costs, the amount must be developed in detention.

If appointments with the embassy are missed or delayed more than three times, the asylum application procedure is terminated and the asylum application is rejected immediately. If a conflict from the country of origin causes a dispute in the initial reception, ethnic groups or minorities are hostile, all troublemakers are immediately deported. If an asylum seeker or refugee commits a criminal offence inland and is sentenced to imprisonment, he or she serves it and is then immediately deported.

Host families can ask the refugee to find another host family. Host families can prevent naturalisation by reporting the refugee and his/her offences to the Ministry of Integration via the Asylum Directory. Once a refugee is reported three times by different families, he or she must move to an Asylum Village and will not be naturalised. If there is already an Asylum Village for his country of origin, he moves there.

9 Switching to the new system

The Ministry of Integration supports the Ministries of Security, Planned Economy and Labour by deporting foreigners. By deporting criminal foreigners, the crime rate is reduced. By deporting social welfare recipients, the social coffers are approved and the Social Villages are not as busy. By deporting more poor and uneducated foreigners, the population is reduced until there are enough jobs and there is full employment.

9.1 Statistical recording

When switching to the new system, the Ministry of Integration must first be established. One of the first official acts is the establishment of the Integration Agency, which initially only has the indoor service. It takes care of the statistical registration of all foreigners and domestic citizens with at least one other nationality living inland.

The place of residence, the extended police clearance certificate and the use of social benefits are to be determined for all foreigners registered. This will prepare the first two waves of deportations of criminal foreigners and foreigners receiving social welfare. After the second wave of deportations, the educational qualifications, monthly income and assets of the remaining foreigners are determined. This prepares the third wave of deportations of poor and uneducated foreigners. If the third wave of deportations is not necessary because there is already full employment, the data is used for integration.

9.2 Withdrawal of domestic nationality

The first law of the Ministry of Integration ensures that all persons with multiple nationalities immediately lose their domestic citizenship. Their domestic identity cards and passports are then invalid and must be handed in at the town hall within one month. If they live abroad, the identity card and passport must be handed in at a consulate or embassy in that foreign country. Those who hold several foreign citizenships may keep them.

After this law, there are only foreigners from Continental Union member states and other countries, So-called third countries. The following measures will only be applied to third-country foreigners. The extension of the measures to Continentals is to take place only in exceptional cases when the measures for third-country foreigners have not been sufficient. In order to simplify the wording, only foreigners will be referred to in the following and no further distinction will be made.

9.3 Stop of the admission

The second law is an immediate freeze on the admission of foreigners from third countries and asylum seekers. The admission freeze applies until the new procedures for immigration and asylum are operational. Ongoing asylum application procedures will be terminated and all asylum applicants will be deported. As soon as the embassies are operational, asylum applications can be submitted there.

9.4 Deportation waves

In the first wave of deportations, all criminal foreigners are deported without exception. Affected are foreigners who have already been in domestic detention or have been sentenced to it, even if only on probation. If these foreigners have already been in detention, they are banned from entering the domestic territory for life. The same applies to all criminal foreigners who were not yet of age at the time of the offence, but who would have received an imprisonment for the offence under adult criminal law. They are deported together with their first-degree family, i.e. parents and underage siblings. This wave of deportations also affects asylum seekers and asylum applicants. In the second wave of deportation, all foreigners who have received social benefits are deported. The persons who have received the most social benefits while living inland are selected first. Last are the foreigners who have only received allowances as social benefits. This includes foreigners who received pensions but were employed in the inland for less than 40 years of their lives on social security. The only social benefit that is not included are benefits to finance training.

In the third wave of deportations, poor and uneducated foreigners are deported. The third wave of deportations continues until there is full employment or a quota of foreigners has been voted on and met. The quota of foreigners is considered to have been met when the national requirement has reached its maximum level. Full employment exists inland as soon as less than 1% of the population of employable age is unemployed and has to live in the Social Villages because there is no work either in the Social Market Economy or in the Free Market Economy. If unemployment inland is still so high after the deportation waves that the Social Villages are overcrowded, the fewer private assets foreigners have, the more they will be deported first. So the last to be deported will be the richest domestic foreigners until full employment is met.

9.4.1 Citizens of Member states of the Continental Union

The deportation waves only extend to foreigners from third countries outside the Continental Union. The Ministry of Foreign Affairs is negotiating a regularisation of the repatriation of criminals and the harmonisation of living standards with the Continental Union member states.

9.5 Compensation payments

Depending on how full the state coffers are, the foreigners are either allowed to keep all of their private assets or have to reimburse social benefits or detention costs in full or in part until their private assets are used up. In the case of pensions, either all pension contributions paid are refunded or the foreigners receive a partial payment or no payment at all.

9.6 Integration of foreigners

All remaining foreigners must report to the citizens' office of their town hall within 3 months of the enactment of the respective law. There they should either announce their departure date or submit a motions for naturalisation in order to receive the permanent residence permit.

9.7 Resettlement of asylum seekers

An Asylum Directory is created using the existing data on all asylum seekers. Based on this data, asylum seekers from the same regions of origin and language regions are housed together. All asylum seekers are relocated to the new Social Villages or the old barracks. If they have been living in mobile containers, these containers are taken away. The asylum seekers build the Social Villages with unemployed people until they are ready. After that, the asylum seekers move on with the containers and build Asylum Villages. The separation of asylum seekers by language and country of origin remains whenever possible.

9.8 Waves of refugees

In the short term, the problem of the waves of refugees is to be solved with United Nations refugee camps in the neighbouring countries of the crisis areas. Preferably, however, countries involved in the war should take in asylum seekers. In the case of Syria, this would be Russia and the USA. In the medium term, it will be possible to take in refugees inland and on the continent, and in the long term there will be no more refugees because the causes of flight will have disappeared.

9.9 Conversion of the old ministries

For the conversion of the old ministries, all departments and units of the old ministries that are changing to this ministry are identified. The organigrams are used to determine whether an entire department and all its units are changing or only individual units. All unsuitable departments and units are dropped. The existing staff adapts its tasks to the new requirements.

Contact form

Dear reader
If you would like to make what you have read come true, in whole or in part, together with other like-minded people, I offer you several possibilities with this contact form. Fill it out, tear out the page and send it by post to:
Andreas Seidl, P.O. Box 1206, 63488 Seligenstadt / Germany

Or send the details to:
Phone: 0049 1522 818 2243 (whatsapp, telegram, signal)
Email: andreas.seidl2022@web.de

Please mark with a cross:
O   I want to found a dynamic People's Party.
O   I want to donate money for implementation.
O   I want contacts with like-minded people in my area.

Forename: ______________________________________

Surname: _______________________________________

Please fill in only the contact option through which a reply should be made.

Street, house no.: __________________________________

Postcode, city, country: ______________________________

Phone: ____

Email address: ____________________________________